100-Day Devotional

Seeking

JESUS

in the
Gospel of Luke

Jesus,

You are my Lord and Savior. Walk alongside me and every reader for the rest of our days.

Fran,

Thank you for being my partner in life and in faith. I love you forever.

Introduction

One of the most notable Bible verses about seeking God is in Jeremiah 29:13:

You shall seek me and find me, when you search for me with all your heart.

But what does seeking Jesus mean, and how do you do it?

In simple terms, seeking Jesus means making him the number one priority in your life.

God gives us an open invitation to an amazing relationship with him. In his fatherly love, he gives us the choice to accept the invitation known as free will. His door is wide open, and it's our choice whether we want to enter.

As Christians, we might be tempted to gloss over this invitation and assume that we're already seeking him because we love him and generally follow the commandments. But there's so much more to seeking Jesus.

I'd like to share two examples to explain the difference between what I call Christianity-by-rote versus seeking Jesus with all your heart. Christianity-by-rote is going through the motions with no real intention behind it. It's doing or saying things out of habit, with hollow words and actions. As a real-life example, in a normal daily exchange with your loved one, you might call out, "Love ya!" while you're rushing out the door. I consider this a loving but hollow gesture. The difference in seeking a genuine relationship would be looking directly into your loved one's eyes and saying, "I love you." The second scenario provides a heartfelt connection.

An example in your prayer life of Christianity-by-rote would be saying the words of the Lord's Prayer, and when you finish, you barely remember what you said. Conversely, when you seek Jesus, you would pray the Lord's Prayer to him as if he were standing right in front of you. Each word would be spoken from your heart, offering it directly to him. When you finish the prayer, it feels like you've just experienced a beautiful union with the Lord.

God wants us to seek him.

The Bible repeatedly mentions seeking the Lord and the joys it brings. The following verses prove that God's will for us is to seek him.

1. You will seek me and find me when you seek me with all your heart. Jeremiah 29:13 (New International Version)

2. But if from there you seek the Lord your God, you will find him if you seek him with all your heart and with all your soul. Deuteronomy 4:29 (NIV)

3. Glory in his holy name; let the hearts of those who seek the Lord rejoice. 1 Chronicles 16:10 (NIV)

4. Now devote your heart and soul to seeking the Lord your God. 1 Chronicles 22:19 (NIV)

5. If you seek him, he will be found by you; 1 Chronicles 28:9 (NIV)

6. He did evil because he had not set his heart on seeking the Lord. 2 Chronicles 12:14 (NIV)

7. The Lord looks down from heaven on all mankind to see if there are any who understand, any who seek God. Psalm 14:2 (NIV)

8. The lions may grow weak and hungry, but those who seek the Lord lack no good thing. Psalm 34:10 (NIV)

How to get closer to Jesus

Seeking Jesus is about pursuing a relationship with him. Christians can get lulled into satisfaction about their relationship with God. Seeking means actively pursuing more.

We reap what we sow in any relationship, and it's no different in our relationship with God. As Christians, we love God. Maybe we spend the final waking minutes of our day in prayer. Maybe we attend church. We (mostly) obey the commandments. God loves us, and we love him.

But when we seek him, we nurture the relationship. We don't say prayers by rote; we feel and mean every word, praying from the heart. We don't plan our shopping list or child's birthday party during the sermon; we actively listen. We make time for God—praying without ceasing. That means throughout the day. We fill our schedule around him. We don't try to squeeze him into our packed schedule. We make time to be still and listen. We meet him in the silence. We read his Word. We make God the priority that he should be. The more that we seek him, the more we come to know his voice.

Does it mean that Jesus loves those who seek him more than those who don't? No. Jesus is by our side, no matter if we have our minds and hearts focused on him or not. The difference is when we seek him, our eyes and ears are opened to what we'd previously been oblivious to see and hear. Seeking opens the door to a more beautiful relationship, and it brings Jesus happiness. He's waiting for each of us just beyond human comprehension. Open your mind and heart and find him there.

How to seek God with your whole heart

Have you ever prayed in desperation for a miracle? Maybe for a dying baby or after a loved one suffered a terrible accident? Seeking Jesus has that type of urgency, power, and relentlessness. The longing to really know Jesus comes from our deepest being. Seeking Jesus is a journey into your heart and soul. It's nothing about the pomp and circumstance that come with showing off to the world what "great Christians" we are.

Just like there is no exact script for seeking a deep relationship with your parent, spouse, or child, we choose the ways that make sense for us when we seek Jesus. The following five examples will get you started on your journey.

5 Ways to Seek Jesus

1 – Open your heart.

As a fair exchange—I speak as to my children—open wide your hearts also. 2 Corinthians 6:13 (NIV)

Seeking is an exercise of the heart. There are almost no external signs when you're seeking. Close your eyes and rest quietly in a peaceful place in your mind's eye.

Feel him there. See him there. Go deep inside and have a beautiful union with God in your heart.

2 – Pray unceasingly.

Pray continually. 1 Thessalonians 5:17 (NIV)

When you seek God, he's your priority. You don't fit a prayer in your day. You fit your day around your prayers. He's the first thought of the day, comes to mind throughout the day, and will be your companion during insomnia. Prayers are spoken from the heart directly to God. If you find yourself saying words without the meaning behind them, keep repeating until you've spoken your prayer by heart. Talk to God as if he's a combination of your parent, best friend, confidante, and therapist who happens to live in your heart.

3 – Be still.

He says, "Be still, and know that I am God." Psalm 46:10 (NIV)

It's in the stillness that Jesus meets us when we seek him. Make sure to give God a chance to answer and guide you. Be intentional about being still. Find a way to get close to God in your mind and heart. Speak to him, honor him, and ask him to join you and guide you. Then stay still in that moment. If your mind drifts to your to-do list (and it will), pull it back and bring God back to the center. Don't be discouraged or stop seeking if you don't get answers or keep getting distracted. He loves you, and he's there waiting for you.

4 – Read the Word.

Consult God's instruction and the testimony of warning. If anyone does not speak according to this word, they have no light of dawn. Isaiah 8:20 (NIV)

God's Word was written to guide us and help us know him. Use it to seek him. When we seek Jesus, we spend time in the Word. We can experience Jesus intimately in Matthew, Mark, Luke, and John. But seeking Jesus is more than simply reading. Seeking happens when we *feel* the message and receive it in our hearts. Walk alongside Jesus in the Gospels. Don't just read the words. See what he saw and feel what he felt. If you find yourself skimming the words, reading without meaning or without it touching your heart, reread it until you make a connection with the words in your heart.

5 – Find community in worship. This can mean church but is also any community of Christians.

For where two or three gather in my name, there am I with them. Matthew 18:20 (NIV)

Seeking takes place in the heart, so it seems illogical that seeking would involve a community. Community matters in seeking because it keeps us accountable, and the presence of Jesus can feel very strong within it. Also, the fellowship and music that generally accompany Christian community can help give us the motivation we need to keep seeking.

What works for me:

First, let me say I'm not a theologian or religious expert. I'm just an average Christian who turned to Jesus in earnest as a young teen, when I was trying to reconcile the drowning of my sixteen-year-old brother when I had been five years old. That experience seemed to ingrain an enormous amount of faith in the afterlife, so much so that one of my well-meaning friends reported me to the high-school counselor after I told her I was looking forward to dying to be able to see heaven. I assured the counselor I wasn't suicidal. I was just communicating my amazement of the afterlife. That excitement and faith have carried into my adulthood, and it is through my own journey of seeking that I've been led to write this book for you. I've prayed for God to give me the words to reach the people he wants me to reach, so this intersection of our lives is what he intended.

Seeking will take on different forms for each of us. Your journey requires you to figure out the best ways of being in God's presence, worshiping him, and listening for his voice.

Try different methods to figure out what works best for you to draw as close to God as you can. The goal is to feel yourself in God's presence, speak to him from your heart there, and listen to what he wants to tell you. Don't give up if you struggle to find his presence. Ask him to help you. He wants to meet you there. He's waiting for you!

How to use this devotional

This devotional will help you seek Jesus by getting to know him personally as you walk beside him through his journey on earth, as told in the book of Luke.

Take yourself back in time and try to imagine experiencing Jesus firsthand through his life and voice in the Gospel verses. The daily, prompted reflections will guide you. Use them to move you along in your seeking journey. Spend time reflecting on your life. Get yourself in God's presence as you reflect on the readings. Pray the daily prayers from your heart. If you find yourself reading without comprehension or intention, go back again more slowly until you're feeling and meaning what you're reading and praying.

Use a supplemental journal to record your thoughts, additional prayers, or make notes for yourself to maximize the impact of your seeking.

May God bless you on this journey and beyond.

But the angel said to him: "Do not be afraid, Zechariah; your prayer has been heard. Your wife Elizabeth will bear you a son, and you are to call him John. He will be a joy and delight to you, and many will rejoice because of his birth, for he will be great in the sight of the Lord. He is never to take wine or other fermented drink, and he will be filled with the Holy Spirit even before he is born. He will bring back many of the people of Israel to the Lord their God. Luke 1:13-16

Reflection:

God's plan for our salvation was conceived and prepared long before Zechariah learned he and Elizabeth were expecting a child in their old age, and after Elizabeth had been deemed barren. John the Baptist's mission was already pre-determined. God's plan for Jesus' arrival on Earth was formed long before Jesus came. We don't often think of Jesus existing in his divinity before he arrived as a human in his mother's womb.

God already knew the decisions men would make that would lead to the crucifixion of his Son. As we try to understand God's plan for our salvation as it's unfolding, it is too large for the human mind to grasp. Yet we understand it enough to be amazed by it. God knew you and me back when he allowed Elizabeth to get pregnant with John the Baptist, and it was all part of his plan for our salvation. How amazing is our God?

Prayer:

Dear Heavenly Father, when Adam and Eve brought sin into the world, you could have let us stumble and fail. We would have each earned a place in eternal hell without your intervention. Instead, you created the perfect plan for our salvation because you love us, even though we're not worthy. I can't grasp the enormity of your love for me, but I pray I can live my life worthy of what you've done for me. I can only do that through your grace. Please help me in the name of Your Son, my Lord and Savior, Jesus Christ. Amen.

The angel said to her, "Don't be afraid, Mary, for you have found favor with God. Behold, you will conceive in your womb and give birth to a son, and shall name him 'Jesus.' He will be great and will be called the Son of the Most High. The Lord God will give him the throne of his father David."... Mary said, "Behold, the servant of the Lord; let it be done to me according to your word." Then the angel departed from her. Luke 1:30-32, 38

Reflection:

What a beautiful plan God had to send his Son into the world as a human to save us! But imagine Mary's shock and confusion when Gabriel came to her. If we think being a young, unwed pregnant lady in today's society is scandalous, imagine the angst Mary might have felt. It could have cost her the relationship with Joseph, as he intended to leave her after he discovered the pregnancy. It certainly would have impacted her reputation and perhaps caused a rift in her family. Mary had almost everything at stake. And yet she answered without hesitation.

Hearing from God is a dream of all who seek him. Maybe He won't send you an angel. Maybe you won't hear him in clear and complete sentences. But when you seek God, listen for his quiet guidance and answers. Mary said yes, without hesitation. Will you?

Prayer:

Dear Lord, help me seek you with all my heart. I want to hear you when you speak to me and to know what your will for my life is. I want to know you. Please open my eyes, ears, mind, and heart to you. Help me be still and find you there. Give me the strength and grace to say "yes" to you without hesitation, like Mary did. As much as

I want your will for me to be easy, I know you will help me accomplish whatever you need from me. Your will be done, Lord. Amen.

When Elizabeth heard Mary's greeting, the baby leaped in her womb; and Elizabeth was filled with the Holy Spirit. She called out with a loud voice and said, "Blessed are you among women, and blessed is the fruit of your womb! Why am I so favored, that the mother of my Lord should come to me? For behold, when the voice of your greeting came into my ears, the baby leaped in my womb for joy! Blessed is she who believed, for there will be a fulfillment of the things which have been spoken to her from the Lord!" Luke 1:41-45

Reflection:

Elizabeth provides us with another powerful example of what walking with the Lord looks like. Elizabeth's baby, John, later known as John the Baptist, leaped in her womb, and Elizabeth was filled with the Holy Spirit when Mary arrived and was pregnant with Jesus. Are you in tune with God's presence in your life? If you were Elizabeth, might you have mistaken the Holy Spirit for simple excitement? Elizabeth's faith is obvious. She helps us understand that in seeking God, we need to be mindful of our spirit, heart, and soul to recognize the ways in which God interacts with us daily.

Prayer:

Dear Lord, you've given us two beautiful examples of women of faith in Mary and Elizabeth. It's easy to ignore the fact that you're calling us to that same level of faith. Please help me remain mindful of Mary and Elizabeth's obedience and faith and realize it's an invitation for me to seek you in the same way. Open my eyes, ears, and heart. Help me let go of my fears, so I can become the devoted servant you'd like me to be. Lead me and I will follow. Amen.

On the eighth day, they came to circumcise the child; and they would have called him Zacharias, after the name of his father. His mother answered, "Not so; but he will be called John." Luke 1:59-60

Reflection:

Elizabeth and Zechariah remained faithful to God's request to name their miracle child John, even though it was customary that the baby would be named after his father. How many times are we grateful for a gift from God, but then we move on with life without giving God what He'd asked of us? It would have been as if Elizabeth and Zechariah had been thankful for their late-in-life pregnancy but then chose to name the child Zechariah to uphold the naming custom of the time. We're always willing to take God's gifts, but we're sometimes less willing to give back to him. As seekers of God, we must remain mindful of putting God's will for our lives before our own desires.

Prayer:

Lord, you have done so many wonderful things for me, and sometimes I take them for granted after the amazement of the moment wears off. Thank you for the example of Elizabeth and Zechariah, who remained faithful to name their child as you'd requested. Help me make your will for my life a priority that I keep in front of me even as I get swept away in daily tasks and habits. I pray you give me the grace to become and remain your faithful servant. In Jesus' name. Amen.

Joseph also went up from Galilee, out of the city of Nazareth, into Judea, to David's city, which is called Bethlehem, because he was of the house and family of David, to enroll himself with Mary, who was pledged to be married to him as wife, being pregnant. While they were there, the day had come for her to give birth. She gave birth to her firstborn son. She wrapped him in bands of cloth and laid him in a feeding trough, because there was no room for them in the inn. (Luke 2:4-7)

Reflection:

We're familiar with the story of Jesus' birth. We've become nonchalant about the fact that he was born in a manger. We take it for granted now. But let's take a mental trip there... Mary and Joseph were traveling in order to be counted in a census. They were traveling while Mary was on the verge of giving birth to her first child! Can you imagine? Can you imagine her fatigue? Her fear? Her discomfort? What about when they arrived only to find there were no rooms available? Wouldn't most women have a meltdown? Sure, they weren't accustomed to fancy accommodations at the time, but to be sleeping in a stable with animals? How would you handle such a test? Might you say, "Seriously, God? I've stuck my neck out to have this baby for you. Can't I at least have a place to sleep?" When you're in the midst of a struggle, how do you respond to God?

Prayer:

Dear Heavenly Father, I don't have the strength and endurance that some of your greatest supporters have had, but through your grace, I'm capable of much more than I realize. Sometimes I fear what you might ask of me, but I lay that fear at your feet now. I know whatever your will for my life is, you'll give me the words, knowledge, and strength to accomplish what you ask of me. I want to do your will. Please guide me. I pray this in Jesus' name. Amen.

Behold, there was a man in Jerusalem whose name was Simeon. This man was righteous and devout, looking for the consolation of Israel, and the Holy Spirit was on him. It had been revealed to him by the Holy Spirit that he should not see death before he had seen the Lord's Christ. He came in the Spirit into the temple. When the parents brought in the child, Jesus, that they might do concerning him according to the custom of the law, then he received him into his arms and blessed God, and said, "Now you are releasing your servant, Master, according to your word, in peace; for my eyes have seen your salvation, which you have prepared before the face of all peoples." Luke 2:25-31

Reflection:

The goal of seeking Jesus is to develop the kind of relationship that Simeon had with him. When we're right with the Lord, when we're in the Word, when we walk with him, and when we seek his will, our minds and hearts become open to see and hear him. He answers us. He speaks to us. If we're attentive and listen to his whispers and pay attention to his gentle nudging, our reward can be like that of Simeon. We can be blessed with a distinctive "knowing" and a recognition of God at work in the world. Hearing God speaking to you or seeing him move in your life is an amazing encounter. It's definitely worth seeking him in earnest.

Prayer:

My Lord and my God, you have been revealing yourself to people for ages, and I pray I can develop that kind of closeness to you. I want to know you and recognize you at work in the world. I want to hear you when you speak to me. Please guide me to become your child whom you can count on to do your will. I can only accomplish that through your grace and your strength. Help me shed all the baggage that keeps me from you. I ask this in the name of Jesus, your Son. Amen.

After three days they found him in the temple, sitting in the middle of the teachers, both listening to them and asking them questions. All who heard him were amazed at his understanding and his answers. When they saw him, they were astonished; and his mother said to him, "Son, why have you treated us this way? Behold, your father and I were anxiously looking for you."

He said to them, "Why were you looking for me? Didn't you know that I must be in my Father's house?" They didn't understand the saying which he spoke to them. Luke 2:46-50

Reflection:

We sometimes forget that Jesus was fully human during his time on earth. Can you imagine the challenges of raising a child who was more obedient to his Holy Father than to his human parents? Especially if you didn't understand fully what was happening. The determined boy stayed behind while his parents left town. Imagine their shock and terror when they realized their son was missing and then searched for him for three days, only to find he was hanging out in the temple without a care in the world! Beyond those frustrations, this glimpse of Jesus' humanity is a beautiful gift to believers. If ever you think he can't possibly understand us or that he can't relate to us, remember his humanity. He *does* understand, and he *can* relate.

Prayer:

Lord God, thank you for this glimpse of Jesus as a human child who frustrated his parents. Sending your Son to save us in human form shows us that you understand our challenges. You have shown your people how much you love us in so many ways, and this is just one more example. I'm also a fallible child. Please have patience with me and continue to love me as I stumble along in my walk with you. Amen.

And Jesus increased in wisdom and stature, and in favor with God and men. Luke 2:52

Reflection:

If you're like me, your heart yearns to know more about the life of the human Jesus. But we're only given a small glimpse. As much as we wish to know more about Jesus' life as a youngster and young man, knowing more isn't necessary, or even relevant, to our Christian walk. We saw that his divinity was recognized among the people, even as a child, and that He was fully human. We have all the information we need. Besides, not having more details about Jesus' early years helps us keep the focus on his adult ministry, which is the cornerstone of everything he accomplished during his time on earth.

Prayer:

Jesus, I'd love to know more about your human side. But that's only because I want to know you more, and it's easier to relate to you as a human. Help me focus instead on the amazing Word that was recorded and not focus on what wasn't. Remind me that everything I need to know about you is right there in the Bible. I love you. Amen.

[The] word of God came to John, the son of Zacharias, in the wilderness. He came into all the region around the Jordan, preaching the baptism of repentance for remission of sins. As it is written in the book of the words of Isaiah the prophet,

The voice of one crying in the wilderness, "Make ready the way of the Lord. Make his paths straight." Luke 3:2-4

Reflection:

When John the Baptist answered God's calling and began his own ministry, he announced the fulfillment of the prophet Isaiah. The Lord was coming, prepare the way! In retrospect, it's easy to understand John's words because we have the benefit of hindsight as evidence of what unfolded after John spoke those words. What would you have thought of him at the time? Would you have changed your life in any way due to his words? Would you have assumed John was just a little odd or quirky and ignored him?

Prayer:

Dear Lord, thank you for the gift of hindsight. There were many contemporaries of John who probably ignored his words, and I might have been one of them. I know you speak to me through other people, like you did through John. Allow me to recognize the signs you give me, whether they're through other people or directly to my heart. Please help me to walk alongside you and lead me back when I stray. I ask this in Jesus' name. Amen.

~ *10* ~

The multitudes asked [John the Baptist], "What then must we do?" He answered them, "He who has two coats, let him give to him who has none. He who has food, let him do likewise."

Tax collectors also came to be baptized, and they said to him, "Teacher, what must we do?" He said to them, "Collect no more than that which is appointed to you."

Soldiers also asked him, saying, "What about us? What must we do?" He said to them, "Extort from no one by violence, neither accuse anyone wrongfully. Be content with your wages." Luke 3:10-14

Reflection:

When John began his ministry of baptism, he was teaching Jesus' message. Baptism is an invitation into God's family, but God also has expectations for his children, in the same way any good parent would. What do those expectations look like for each of us? As John described, each of us is faced with differing circumstances, life challenges, and personal strengths and weaknesses. Being generous, honest, kind, and content are John's universal words that still speak to each of us today. What holds you back from being generous, honest, kind, or content in your daily life? Have you aced all of those? Great! In what other ways are you falling short? These are the things that Jesus asks you to put aside to follow him. No more excuses.

Prayer:

Dear Holy Father, thank you for accepting me into your family. It's the most beautiful gift I could ever receive. Help me to become the child you've called me to be. Give me strength and humility to put aside the selfish things that I hold tighter than honesty, generosity, kindness, and contentment. Please draw me back to you when I let my worldly cares and desires separate me from your will. I ask this through your Son, Jesus Christ. Amen.

Now when all the people were baptized, Jesus also had been baptized and was praying. The sky was opened, and the Holy Spirit descended in a bodily form like a dove on him; and a voice came out of the sky, saying, "You are my beloved Son. In you I am well pleased." Luke 3:21-22

Reflection:

Most Christians long for precious occasions when God our Father breaks through the invisible barrier that separates Heaven from Earth. Throughout the Bible, we experience a few monumental moments, such as the one at Jesus' baptism. When the Holy Spirit descended upon Jesus during his baptism and God literally spoke to the crowd, it had to be a life-changing experience for anyone in attendance. But how can we hold onto the wonder of that moment through the written Word? Imagine how desperately God wanted to reach his people that He made himself known in such a personal way. How much more can He do to show people He not only exists but has sent his Son into our world to save us? May this example of God speaking openly to humanity help restore your faith in times of doubt.

Prayer:

Lord, if only I could have witnessed your majesty on that day of Jesus' baptism... Not because I lack faith, but because I long to see you, hear you, and be close to you. Remind me of the many ways you show me love when my faith is weak or when I feel unworthy of your love. Help me find you in everyday ways in my own life. Speak loudly if I'm not listening. Please don't give up on me. I love you. In Jesus' name. Amen.

Jesus himself, when he began to teach, was about thirty years old...
Luke 3:23

Reflection:

It's hard to imagine the difficulties Jesus faced living as fully human and fully divine. Our little glimpse of him as a child staying behind in the temple when his parents left town shows us that he already knew he was of God. As he grew into adulthood, when did he fully understand his purpose? As fully human, Jesus may have been fearful of what was to come, in the same way we might fear the calling God has for us. Will we have to leave our family or friends behind? Will we be asked to do a task we dread? Will God's will for us be more difficult or painful than we'd want to bear? God prepared Jesus for thirty years before he began his ministry. So, too, will he prepare us for ours. There is no reason to fear.

Prayer:

Jesus, thank you for taking human form to save us and setting an example of what it truly means to follow God's will. Through the example of your ministry, you teach us that it's not about fanfare or popularity. Lead me in my quest to discern and follow your will. Help me to change my life and to reach the people you'd like me to reach, even if it's only within my family or friends. Help me to be content with a small calling and to be capable of handling a larger calling. I want to use my life to bring people to you. Guide me and nudge me to follow. My life is yours. Amen.

Jesus, full of the Holy Spirit, returned from the Jordan and was led by the Spirit into the wilderness for forty days, being tempted by the devil. He ate nothing in those days. Afterward, when they were completed, he was hungry. The devil said to him, "If you are the Son of God, command this stone to become bread." Jesus answered him, saying, "It is written, 'Man shall not live by bread alone, but by every word of God.'"

The devil, leading him up on a high mountain, showed him all the kingdoms of the world in a moment of time. The devil said to him, "I will give you all this authority and their glory, for it has been delivered to me, and I give it to whomever I want. If you therefore will worship before me, it will all be yours." Jesus answered him, "Get behind me, Satan! For it is written, 'You shall worship the Lord your God, and you shall serve him only.'"

He led him to Jerusalem and set him on the pinnacle of the temple, and said to him, "If you are the Son of God, cast yourself down from here, for it is written, 'He will put his angels in charge of you, to guard you; and, 'On their hands they will bear you up, lest perhaps you dash your foot against a stone.'" Jesus answering, said to him, "It has been said, 'You shall not tempt the Lord your God.'" Luke 4:1-12

Reflection:

Jesus' time in the desert is a powerful example for us. He fasted for forty days! For most humans, fasting for one day is a challenge. Imagine how his hunger would have weakened his physical condition and probably his mental condition as well. But we see by his responses to the devil's temptation that his spiritual strength remained stronger than ever. How can we resist temptation, even when we're beat down, spiritually hungry, mentally tired, or emotionally discouraged? We can always stay grounded in the Word of God, as Jesus did. No matter our physical, mental, or spiritual condition, the Word remains our "true north."

Prayer:

Lord, many worldly things try to weaken my relationship with you. Help me realize the temptations in my life are Satan calling me away from you. Whether it be addiction, overindulging, vanity, self-righteousness, lying, or other sins, please point me back to you, my "true north." Speak to me through your Word and help me to stay on the path that leads to eternal salvation. Give me the strength to say NO to the world and YES to you. Jesus' name. Amen.

All testified about him and wondered at the gracious words which proceeded out of his mouth; and they said, "Isn't this Joseph's son?" He said to them, "Doubtless you will tell me this proverb, 'Physician, heal yourself! Whatever we have heard done at Capernaum, do also here in your hometown.'" He said, "Most certainly I tell you, no prophet is acceptable in his hometown.

They were all filled with wrath in the synagogue as they heard these things. They rose up, threw him out of the city, and led him to the brow of the hill that their city was built on, that they might throw him off the cliff. But he, passing through the middle of them, went his way. Luke 4:22-24, 28-30

Reflection:

Everyone loved Jesus... until he started saying things they didn't like. Here we see people in his hometown turning against him and driving him out of town, intending to harm him. We're fortunate to live in a world where most of us aren't physically harmed for speaking out for Jesus, so we don't really need to be concerned about being thrown off a cliff. But following Jesus can mean sticking our necks out. Jesus' way isn't the popular way. His way runs counter to much of today's society. We need to trust that when we support Jesus, we'll survive any fallout. God will protect us from harm.

Prayer:

Dear Heavenly Father, sometimes I get complacent in my walk with you. I tend to keep our relationship in my heart and my head because it's easier and safer than speaking out on your behalf. Give me the courage to be your voice. Tell me when you want me to speak out and give me the words to say. Help me trust that you'll protect me from any repercussions. I pray I can be your good servant, and I know with your guidance, I can. I ask this in Jesus' name. Amen.

~ *15* ~

In the synagogue there was a man who had a spirit of an unclean demon; and he cried out with a loud voice, saying, "Ah! what have we to do with you, Jesus of Nazareth? Have you come to destroy us? I know who you are: the Holy One of God!" Jesus rebuked him, saying, "Be silent and come out of him!" When the demon had thrown him down in the middle of them, he came out of him, having done him no harm. Amazement came on all and they spoke together, one with another, saying, "What is this word? For with authority and power he commands the unclean spirits, and they come out!" News about him went out into every place of the surrounding region. Luke 4:33-37

Reflection:

Jesus became the talk of the town as he began his public ministry. It was very clear that anyone who witnessed Jesus' acts knew they were out of the ordinary, thus his reputation quickly spread throughout the area. Everyone who knew him then and since his death have all agreed he was a special man. Many say he was simply a prophet. The people of that time couldn't have imagined that the man who spoke with such authority and power would be the source of the most significant spiritual divide the world would ever see—the Messiah they'd been awaiting.

Prayer:

Jesus, since the day you roamed the earth, people have questioned and debated your identity. I thank you for the faith I've been given to believe in your divinity. When doubt wants to creep in, let your Word keep it at bay. Use me to bring your Good News to nonbelievers and boost the faith of other believers. You are my Lord and my God forever and ever. Amen.

When it was day, he departed and went into an uninhabited place and the multitudes looked for him, and came to him, and held on to him, so that he wouldn't go away from them. But he said to them, "I must preach the good news of God's Kingdom to the other cities also. For this reason I have been sent." Luke 4:42-43

Reflection:

As Jesus became well known and loved, people begged him to stay with them, just as we would when we love someone. How flattering and tempting it must have been for him to remain at the places where he was loved and wanted. But Jesus never took the easy way. It wasn't about his ego, where he felt comfortable, or even what his own desires were. He knew he was living out his Father's will and was determined to fulfill what needed to be done. His example reminds us to keep moving forward when we find ourselves in a comfortable place. Seeking Jesus requires climbing a high mountain. The quest is long, but it is worth the climb.

Prayer:

Dear Lord, I like to stop when I reach a comfortable spot. The temptation to become complacent is very strong. Please give me the strength to keep seeking you without ceasing. Nudge me when I rest for too long. Remind me that there's always room for me to grow and that there are always ways I can continue to bring your Word to people. I know when I leave my comfort zone, you're right by my side, and that's all I need. In Jesus' name, I pray for your guidance and protection. Amen.

Now while the multitude pressed on him and heard the word of God, he was standing by the lake of Gennesaret. He saw two boats standing by the lake, but the fishermen had gone out of them and were washing their nets. He entered into one of the boats, which was Simon's, and asked him to put out a little from the land. He sat down and taught the multitudes from the boat. When he had finished speaking, he said to Simon, "Put out into the deep and let down your nets for a catch." Simon answered him, "Master, we worked all night and caught nothing; but at your word I will let down the net." When they had done this, they caught a great multitude of fish, and their net was breaking. They beckoned to their partners in the other boat, that they should come and help them. They came and filled both boats, so that they began to sink. But Simon Peter, when he saw it, fell down at Jesus' knees, saying, "Depart from me, for I am a sinful man, Lord." For he was amazed, and all who were with him, at the catch of fish which they had caught; and so also were James and John, sons of Zebedee, who were partners with Simon. Jesus said to Simon, "Don't be afraid. From now on you will be catching people alive." When they had brought their boats to land, they left everything, and followed him. Luke 5:1-11

Reflection:

As Jesus' reputation grew, the number of people who flocked to see him grew, too. Being out on the water gave him a good vantage point from which to speak to the crowd. It also gave him an opportunity to begin calling his disciples. We forget that Simon, James, John, and the others had lives of their own. They had jobs, families, and other responsibilities. They had obligations and commitments.

Yet when Jesus asked Simon to drop his nets after a fruitless night of fishing, Simon obliged without hesitation. After their catch, the men dropped everything to follow Jesus. Imagine how incredibly powerful the experience must have been for the men to leave their whole lives behind at a moment's notice. Are you willing to let go of "things" in your life that separate you from God's calling? Do you oblige when Jesus asks you to drop your net?

Prayer:

Dear Heavenly Father, I trust that anything you ask of me is possible, and it has nothing to do with my own skills or knowledge. If you ask me to do it, you'll make sure I can accomplish it. I want to follow you like Simon and the other apostles did. I pray to have the same unwavering commitment to you. Lord, tell me where to cast my net. I ask this in the name of my Lord, Jesus. Amen.

While he was in one of the cities, behold, there was a man full of leprosy. When he saw Jesus, he fell on his face and begged him, saying, "Lord, if you want to, you can make me clean." He stretched out his hand and touched him, saying, "I want to. Be made clean." Immediately the leprosy left him. He commanded him to tell no one, "But go your way and show yourself to the priest, and offer for your cleansing according to what Moses commanded, for a testimony to them." But the report concerning him spread much more, and great multitudes came together to hear and to be healed by him of their infirmities. But he withdrew himself into the desert and prayed. Luke 5:12-16

Reflection:

Jesus healed those who had faith, and he asks the same faith of us today. If he can heal the sick and if he can fill fishing nets in water that had no fish, how can we not trust that he can move mountains in our own lives? When we pray in earnest, God will answer. It's not always the answer we're hoping for, but his will is perfect, even when it doesn't feel like it and doesn't align with our wishes. When he helps us, he asks us to give testimony. How do you give testimony for God's goodness in your life?

Prayer:

Lord, we see miraculous healings in today's world. Many times, it's attributed to modern medicine. But the interviews of the doctors who say there is no medical explanation for a patient's recovery never seem to make the news highlights. You're at work all around us. Help me to see and believe and give testimony. I pray always in the name of Jesus. Amen.

On one of those days, he was teaching; and there were Pharisees and teachers of the law sitting by who had come out of every village of Galilee, Judea, and Jerusalem. The power of the Lord was with him to heal them. Behold, men brought a paralyzed man on a cot, and they sought to bring him in to lay before Jesus. Not finding a way to bring him in because of the multitude, they went up to the housetop and let him down through the tiles with his cot into the middle before Jesus. Seeing their faith, he said to him, "Man, your sins are forgiven you." The scribes and the Pharisees began to reason, saying, "Who is this who speaks blasphemies? Who can forgive sins, but God alone?"

But Jesus, perceiving their thoughts, answered them, "Why are you reasoning so in your hearts? Which is easier to say, 'Your sins are forgiven you,' or to say, 'Arise and walk'? But that you may know that the Son of Man has authority on earth to forgive sins," he said to the paralyzed man, "I tell you, arise, take up your cot, and go to your house." Immediately he rose up before them, and took up that which he was laying on, and departed to his house, glorifying God. Amazement took hold on all, and they glorified God. They were filled with fear, saying, "We have seen strange things today." Luke 5:17-26

Reflection:

Here's another healing miracle and an example of the lengths to which the friends of the paralyzed man went to get Jesus' attention. Besides the healing, we also see Jesus revealing himself as being able to forgive sins. We can see why the Pharisees and teachers of the law thought He was blaspheming. In hindsight, we now know that Jesus is the Son of God, so it's easier for us to accept God's miraculous presence on earth than it was for the Pharisees. Jesus told them He had the authority to forgive sins, and as such, revealed his whole purpose of humanity's salvation. But no one at the time could comprehend it. However, they certainly understood the enormity of a paralyzed man being cured on the spot. God knows that the heavenly Kingdom is beyond human comprehension, so He delivers messages to us in everyday ways that we are able to understand, if only we choose to listen.

Prayer:

Dear Heavenly Father, thank you for all the miracles you perform in our world. More importantly, thank you for forgiving our sins, which allows us to spend eternity with you in Heaven. I don't want to be close-minded, like the Pharisees. Open my eyes to you and help me in my times of doubt. Help me hold tight to your majesty and your promises for your people. I ask this in the name of Jesus. Amen.

After these things he went out and saw a tax collector named Levi [Matthew] sitting at the tax office, and said to him, "Follow me!" He left everything, and rose up and followed him. Levi made a great feast for him in his house. There was a great crowd of tax collectors and others who were reclining with them. Their scribes and the Pharisees murmured against his disciples, saying, "Why do you eat and drink with the tax collectors and sinners?" Jesus answered them, "Those who are healthy have no need for a physician, but those who are sick do. I have not come to call the righteous, but sinners, to repentance." Luke 5:27-32

Reflection:

Levi, whom we've come to know as Matthew, may have been a sinner by the standards of the time, but he left everything and followed Jesus without hesitation. As we're all sinners, Jesus gives us the same invitation. Do you follow without hesitation? Do you celebrate Jesus as Levi did? Levi was transformed, just as we are given the chance to follow and transform. The offer of salvation is extended to all of us. Do you accept it as freely and willingly as Levi did?

Prayer:

Lord, I'm a sinner. I believe that you came to earth to offer me eternal salvation, and I pray that I can change my ways and follow you as righteously as Levi did. Help me not to judge others as the Pharisees did. Help me run my own race to you and help others along the way, rather than casting stones at them. Use me as an instrument to bring people to you. I ask this in the holy name of Jesus Christ. Amen.

In these days, [Jesus] went out to the mountain to pray, and he continued all night in prayer to God. When it was day, he called his disciples, and from them he chose twelve, whom he also named apostles: Simon, whom he also named Peter; Andrew, his brother; James; John; Philip; Bartholomew; Matthew; Thomas; James the son of Alphaeus; Simon who was called the Zealot; Judas the son of James [aka Thaddeus]; and Judas Iscariot, who also became a traitor. Luke 6:12-16

Reflection:

Jesus is God, yet when he was human, he still prayed to God the Father. He spent the entire night praying, and apparently, he was discerning God's will, because afterward he chose his twelve apostles. How much time do you spend in prayer? How much of that time is spent listening? When we truly seek to know God, time spent in quiet reflection or being still and waiting for him can result in the most rewarding and life-changing encounters. Make sure you give God a chance to speak to you, whether it be through images, actual words, or thoughts in your heart. Listen closely or you might miss it.

Prayer:

Dear Heavenly Father, Jesus set many examples for us, and his hours spent in prayer are certainly a notable example. It's also an area I sometimes cut short. Give me the discipline to set aside time with you and not allow myself to get so swept away in daily life that you become last priority. Help me to pray without ceasing and to seek your will and listen for your answers. Lord, I cherish the times I find you in the quietness of my soul. Please meet me there and reveal yourself to me. Guide me to living out my life according to your will, as Jesus did. I love you. Amen.

He lifted up his eyes to his disciples, and said: "Blessed are you who are poor, for God's Kingdom is yours. Blessed are you who hunger now, for you will be filled. Blessed are you who weep now, for you will laugh. Blessed are you when men hate you, and when they exclude and mock you, and throw out your name as evil, for the Son of Man's sake. Rejoice in that day and leap for joy, for behold, your reward is great in heaven, for their fathers did the same thing to the prophets. But woe to you who are rich! For you have received your consolation. Woe to you, you who are full now, for you will be hungry. Woe to you who laugh now, for you will mourn and weep. Woe, when men speak well of you, for their fathers did the same thing to the false prophets." Luke 6:20-26

Reflection:

Jesus said many things that people couldn't understand at the time. Thankfully, we have the benefit of hindsight to help us understand these instructions for how to live our lives pleasing to God. In these beautiful promises known as the "Beatitudes," Jesus taught us that the pain and sorrows we have in life will someday, somehow, turn into blessings. He also cautions us that living life for worldly rewards will lead to much regret later. Each day, we make choices about how we'll spend eternity. God gave us free will. Where are our choices leading?

Prayer:

Lord, thank you for sending Jesus to save us. He taught us so much about how to live our lives to be pleasing to you, and the Beatitudes are just one example. Help me live according to your will, in humble service of others and living boldly in the name of Jesus, no matter the consequences. Help me live my life as an example to others about what it means to delay gratification in service, so that I might reap your eternal blessings. With love always, from your faithful servant. Amen

But I tell you who hear: love your enemies, do good to those who hate you, bless those who curse you, and pray for those who mistreat you. To him who strikes you on the cheek, offer also the other; and from him who takes away your cloak, don't withhold your coat also. Give to everyone who asks you, and don't ask him who takes away your goods to give them back again. As you would like people to do to you, do exactly so to them. If you love those who love you, what credit is that to you? For even sinners love those who love them. If you do good to those who do good to you, what credit is that to you? For even sinners do the same. If you lend to those from whom you hope to receive, what credit is that to you? Even sinners lend to sinners, to receive back as much. But love your enemies, and do good, and lend, expecting nothing back; and your reward will be great, and you will be children of the Most High; for he is kind toward the unthankful and evil. Therefore be merciful, even as your Father is also merciful. Luke 6:27-36

Reflection:

Jesus often talked about the importance of love. Not only is loving one another of the utmost importance, but *loving when it's hard to love* is the real challenge. Even sinners love those who love them; there's no challenge in that. Jesus challenges us to show Godly love. He gave us many examples by loving and forgiving those who mocked, beat, and even killed him. When we compare our circumstances to Jesus's, it's pretty clear that loving and forgiving someone who's disappointed or hurt us is doable. But it's our choice. How much do we choose to hang on to the hurt, pain, or embarrassment over pleasing God?

Prayer:

Jesus, you set the ultimate example of love and forgiveness for us. Give me the strength to let go of the hurt and pain from being abused, neglected, betrayed, or taken advantage of. Even though my heart was broken or my ego bruised, I now lay the grudges at your feet. It's only through your strength and grace that I can let go of the pain and move forward with my life, free of that heavy weight. Once I'm no longer carrying that burden, I can open myself up to living life fully and according to your will. I ask this in your holy name. Amen.

~ *24* ~

Why do you see the speck of chaff (sawdust) that is in your brother's eye, but don't consider the beam (plank) that is in your own eye? Or how can you tell your brother, "Brother, let me remove the speck of chaff that is in your eye," when you yourself don't see the beam that is in your own eye! You hypocrite! First remove the beam from your own eye, and then you can see clearly to remove the speck of chaff that is in your brother's eye. Luke 6:41-42

Reflection:

Too many people fall into the trap of focusing on other people's imperfections. Unfortunately, Christians are no exception. We use excuses like, "Jesus spoke against sinners, and He said we need to speak out." True, we're called to profess the Good News and encourage people in their walk with God. But never forget that we're all sinners. Keep yourself in check by taking a serious look in the mirror and removing any "planks" from your eye. If you focus on tidying up your spiritual flaws, you'll end up having more Godly influence on people than you would by pointing out their errors.

Prayer:

God, sometimes the sins of other sinners seem so obvious that I become self-righteous. Please remind me that no one except Jesus was without sin. I ask for the humility and grace to see my own sins before seeing those of others. Let me become a humble example for other Christians so that my life will draw people to you rather than push them away. I pray that as I interact with other Christians and non-Christians, you will give me the right words to use for the glory of your Kingdom. Amen.

For there is no good tree that produces rotten fruit, nor again a rotten tree that produces good fruit. For each tree is known by its own fruit. For people don't gather figs from thorns, nor do they gather grapes from a bramble bush. The good man out of the good treasure of his heart brings out that which is good, and the evil man out of the evil treasure of his heart brings out that which is evil, for out of the abundance of the heart, his mouth speaks. Luke 6:43-45

Reflection:

The mouth is the expression of the heart, so a good way to assess the condition of someone's heart is to pay attention to their words. We can all be on our best behavior when we want to be. We all have good days. But what happens when things go wrong? When someone upsets us, when we're all alone and angry, how do we react? If you were an independent observer of yourself, how would you describe your words and reactions? They are an indication of the good or evil stored in your heart. Is it a pretty or noble picture? Terrific! Is it a vile, evil mess? If so, then take heed. Draw closer to Jesus by seeking him in earnest, and He will help turn your heart into a place of love and light.

Prayer:

Dear Lord, you already know the condition of my heart. You already know what I choose to show others and what I try to conceal. You see it all. The evil that's stored there prevents me from living your will fully. It keeps barriers between me and my loved ones. Please soften the hard spots in my heart and help me become the obedient child you'd like me to be. Through your grace, my words can become a light for your people. Please let me become a person who draws people to you by my example and my words. I pray in Jesus' name. Amen.

After [Jesus] had finished speaking in the hearing of the people, he entered into Capernaum. A certain centurion's servant, who was dear to him, was sick and at the point of death. When he heard about Jesus, he sent to him elders of the Jews, asking him to come and save his servant. When they came to Jesus, they begged him earnestly, saying, "He is worthy for you to do this for him, for he loves our nation, and he built our synagogue for us." Jesus went with them. When he was now not far from the house, the centurion sent friends to him, saying to him, "Lord, don't trouble yourself, for I am not worthy for you to come under my roof. Therefore I didn't even think myself worthy to come to you; but say the word, and my servant will be healed. For I also am a man placed under authority, having under myself soldiers. I tell this one, 'Go!' and he goes; and to another, 'Come!' and he comes; and to my servant, 'Do this,' and he does it." When Jesus heard these things, he marveled at him, and turned and said to the multitude who followed him, "I tell you, I have not found such great faith, no, not in Israel." Those who were sent, returning to the house, found that the servant who had been sick was well. Luke 7:1-10

Reflection:

Much of Jesus' ministry involved rewarding those who showed great faith. In this case, even Jesus was amazed that this man, who had great authority in the world, would humble himself and feel unworthy of Jesus entering his home. How do we keep such humility in our own lives? How do we remember that any successes we achieve in life are only through the grace of God? How do we keep God as a top priority even when life is humming along smoothly? We tend to turn to Jesus when we face difficulties. But when we keep seeking him even in times of plenty, we will remain genuinely humble and amaze Jesus with our great faith.

Prayer:

Jesus, it's so easy to become absorbed in the successes in my life, no matter how small they are. When I lose sight of you and begin to feel independent of you, please lead me back. Help me remain humble. Remind me that you're in control. I am nothing without you. I need you always because you are my Lord and Savior. Amen.

Soon afterwards, [Jesus] went to a city called Nain. Many of his disciples, along with a great multitude, went with him. Now when he came near to the gate of the city, behold, one who was dead was carried out, the only born son of his mother, and she was a widow. Many people of the city were with her. When the Lord saw her, he had compassion on her and said to her, "Don't cry." He came near and touched the coffin, and the bearers stood still. He said, "Young man, I tell you, arise!" He who was dead sat up and began to speak. Then he gave him to his mother.

Fear took hold of all, and they glorified God, saying, "A great prophet has arisen among us!" and, "God has visited his people!" This report went out concerning him in the whole of Judea and in all the surrounding region. Luke 7:11-17

Reflection:

Jesus brought many people back to life over the course of his ministry. But many people also died without being brought back. How does God choose, even today, when a miracle is granted? There are many believers who pray for healing for their loved ones, but we can't expect every request for physical healing to be granted. What we *can* learn from Jesus' example is that everything is possible with God. When we see a person die, it seems impossible that they could come back to life. When Jesus showed us this miracle in his Word, and many other examples, he was giving doubters a glimpse of the unimaginable power of God at work.

Prayer:

Dear Lord, the extent of your power is beyond my comprehension. Help me become observant of the miracles happening every day around me. Every miracle gives me a glimpse of your amazing love. May your miracles be the proof that nonbelievers need to turn to you. I pray this in Jesus' holy name. Amen.

~ *28* ~

The disciples of John told him about all these things. John, calling to himself two of his disciples, sent them to Jesus, saying, "Are you the one who is coming, or should we look for another?" When the men had come to him, they said, "John the Baptizer has sent us to you, saying, 'Are you he who comes, or should we look for another?'"

In that hour [Jesus] cured many of diseases and plagues and evil spirits; and to many who were blind he gave sight. Jesus answered them, "Go and tell John the things which you have seen and heard: that the blind receive their sight, the lame walk, the lepers are cleansed, the deaf hear, the dead are raised up, and the poor have good news preached to them. Blessed is he who finds no occasion for stumbling in me."

When John's messengers had departed, he began to tell the multitudes about John, "What did you go out into the wilderness to see? A reed shaken by the wind? But what did you go out to see? A man clothed in soft clothing? Behold, those who are gorgeously dressed and live delicately are in kings' courts. But what did you go out to see? A prophet? Yes, I tell you, and much more than a prophet. This is he of whom it is written, 'Behold, I send my messenger before your face, who will prepare your way before you.' "For I tell you, among those who are born of women there is not a greater prophet than John the Baptizer; yet he who is least in God's Kingdom is greater than he." When all the people and the tax collectors heard this, they declared God to be just, having been baptized with John's baptism. Luke 7:18-29

Reflection:

Even with his important role in Jesus' ministry, John the Baptist didn't fully grasp who Jesus was and how important John's role would be for the first believers: the first Christians. Even when Jesus explained to the people how John was fulfilling prophecies, many people chose not to believe. We can use these passages as examples to seek Jesus and trust that he will guide our lives for his purpose, if we let him. Even when we're blind to his plan, keep trusting. He already knows the perfect ending. All he needs is our obedience, like John's.

Prayer:

Jesus, I trust in you and your perfect plan. Please use me to reveal your grace and goodness to your people. Give me the guidance, words, and actions to accomplish your will for me. With you beside me, I can accomplish anything you ask of me. I love you. Amen.

One of the Pharisees invited [Jesus] to eat with him. He entered into the Pharisee's house and sat at the table. Behold, a woman in the city who was a sinner, when she knew that he was reclining in the Pharisee's house, brought an alabaster jar of ointment. Standing behind at his feet weeping, she began to wet his feet with her tears, and she wiped them with the hair of her head, kissed his feet, and anointed them with the ointment. Now when the Pharisee who had invited him saw it, he said to himself, "This man, if he were a prophet, would have perceived who and what kind of woman this is who touches him, that she is a sinner."

Jesus answered him, "Simon, I have something to tell you." He said, "Teacher, say on." "A certain lender had two debtors. The one owed five hundred denarii (ancient Roman coin), and the other fifty. When they couldn't pay, he forgave them both. Which of them therefore will love him most?" Simon answered, "He, I suppose, to whom he forgave the most."

He said to him, "You have judged correctly." Turning to the woman, he said to Simon, "Do you see this woman? I entered into your house, and you gave me no water for my feet, but she has wet my feet with her tears, and wiped them with the hair of her head. You gave me no kiss, but she, since the time I came in, has not ceased to kiss my feet. You didn't anoint my head with oil, but she has anointed my feet with ointment. Therefore I tell you, her sins, which are many, are forgiven, for she loved much. But one to whom little is forgiven, loves little." He said to her, "Your sins are forgiven." Luke 7:36-50

Reflection:

Jesus shows us here that He's only looking for our best, even if it's only tears. He's not expecting us to save the world on his behalf. He's expecting us to do our part for him in our little place within the world. When we have riches, such as expensive perfume, Jesus wants that, too. He wants all of us. He wants us to offer everything to his glory. He wants us to lay it all at his feet.

Prayer:

Dear Heavenly Father, I often want my impact in the world to be greater than it is. I want to be used in "bigger" ways, to reach more people, to bring about change in the world. But you've told us that you only need us to offer you what we have. Help me to be content with my gifts, with where you've asked me to be, and just live my life giving it all to you. I ask this through Jesus Christ. Amen.

~ *30* ~

When a great multitude came together and people from every city were coming to [Jesus], he spoke by a parable: "The farmer went out to sow his seed. As he sowed, some fell along the road, and it was trampled under foot, and the birds of the sky devoured it. Other seed fell on the rock, and as soon as it grew, it withered away, because it had no moisture. Other fell amid the thorns, and the thorns grew with it and choked it. Other fell into the good ground and grew and produced one hundred times as much fruit." As he said these things, he called out, "He who has ears to hear, let him hear!" Then his disciples asked him, "What does this parable mean?"

He said, "To you it is given to know the mysteries of God's Kingdom, but to the rest it is given in parables, that 'seeing they may not see, and hearing they may not understand.' Now the parable is this: The seed is the word of God. Those along the road are those who hear; then the devil comes and takes away the word from their heart, that they may not believe and be saved. Those on the rock are they who, when they hear, receive the word with joy; but these have no root. They believe for a while, then fall away in time of temptation. What fell among the thorns, these are those who have heard, and as they go on their way they are choked with cares, riches, and pleasures of life; and they bring no fruit to maturity. Those in the good ground, these are those who with an honest and good heart, having heard the word, hold it tightly, and produce fruit with perseverance." Luke 8:4-15

Reflection:

Growing faith is not as simple as waiting for it to happen. It requires active participation. When we don't seek Jesus, we end up pushing God aside during the good times. We get angry at him during life's challenges. But when we make a concerted effort to seek him, we make him a priority, even when our "to-do" plates are overflowing. Nurture your faith with the same passionate intensity that you'd have in tending to a dying child or spouse. Make it non-negotiable on your priority list. Many other distractions are vying for attention. If you don't seek God with all your heart, your relationship will likely fade away.

Prayer:

Lord, the only way I can nurture my seed of faith is by seeking you. Remind me to look to you through the good times and hard times. Keep revealing yourself to me when I seek you. It fills my heart with joy when I feel you with me and hear your voice. Stay by my side. I need you. Amen.

[Jesus'] mother and brothers came to him, and they could not come near him for the crowd. Some people told him, "Your mother and your brothers stand outside, desiring to see you." But he answered them, "My mother and my brothers are these who hear the word of God and do it." Luke 8:19-21

Reflection:

Most of us love our family members dearly. We make vows with our spouses to love and cherish them for the rest of our days. It feels harsh that Jesus dissed his mother and brothers. It's a difficult concept when we look at it in human terms. But when we seek Jesus, He's truly all that matters. It doesn't mean we don't love our family members. It means that, given a choice, seekers choose him over family members. It means not letting any human come in between your relationship with God. Your spouse doesn't want to attend church? It shouldn't stop you. Your mother has turned from her faith? Don't let it diminish your faith. When you seek Jesus and your relationship with him is your highest priority, it supersedes anything in this world. Anything.

Prayer:

Lord, I love my family and I love you. I choose you over anyone and everything. You are the heavenly Creator and King and worthy of my utmost love and devotion. Help me never to let anyone or anything ever separate me from you. I pray in the name of Jesus, my Savior. Amen.

Now on one of those days, [Jesus] entered into a boat, himself and his disciples, and he said to them, "Let's go over to the other side of the lake." So they launched out. But as they sailed, he fell asleep. A wind storm came down on the lake, and they were taking on dangerous amounts of water. They came to him and awoke him, saying, "Master, Master, we are dying!" He awoke and rebuked the wind and the raging of the water; then they ceased, and it was calm. He said to them, "Where is your faith?" Being afraid, they marveled, saying to one another, "Who is this then, that he commands even the winds and the water, and they obey him?" Luke 8:22-25

Reflection:

Have you ever experienced a near-drowning? It's terrifying. Perhaps that's why Jesus used such an extreme example to prove to his disciples that there was no reason to fear. Does the miracle he performed mean he'll save us from every harm, too? No. But it means that in Jesus, we can trust the outcome will be okay, even when all we can see is raging water. Jesus wants us to have faith. Faith is easy when life is good. But how do we keep faith strong when the water is raging? Seek him during the good times, and it will be easier to find him during the challenges.

Prayer:

Dear Lord, there are so many scary things about life, like illness, financial crises, accidents, and death. I know that with you, I have the strength to handle anything that comes my way, but I still get afraid sometimes. I pray for your strength to sustain me when I want to crumble. Comfort me and my loved ones when we're terrified and brokenhearted. Help us to rely on you to calm the storm and put our broken pieces back together. I ask this in Jesus' name. Amen.

~ *33* ~

Then they arrived at the country of the Gadarenes, which is opposite Galilee. When Jesus stepped ashore, a certain man out of the city who had demons for a long time met him. He wore no clothes, and didn't live in a house, but in the tombs. When he saw Jesus, he cried out and fell down before him, and with a loud voice said, "What do I have to do with you, Jesus, you Son of the Most High God? I beg you, don't torment me!" For Jesus was commanding the unclean spirit to come out of the man. For the unclean spirit had often seized the man. He was kept under guard and bound with chains and fetters. Breaking the bonds apart, he was driven by the demon into the desert.

Jesus asked him, "What is your name?" He said, "Legion," for many demons had entered into him. They begged him that he would not command them to go into the abyss. Now there was there a herd of many pigs feeding on the mountain, and they begged him that he would allow them to enter into those. Then he allowed them. The demons came out of the man and entered into the pigs, and the herd rushed down the steep bank into the lake and were drowned. When those who fed them saw what had happened, they fled and told it in the city and in the country. People went out to see what had happened. They came to Jesus and found the man from whom the demons had gone out, sitting at Jesus' feet, clothed and in his right mind; and they were afraid. Those who saw it told them how he who had been possessed by demons was healed. All the people of the surrounding country of the Gadarenes asked him to depart from them, for they were very much afraid. Then he entered into the boat and returned.

But the man from whom the demons had gone out begged him that he might go with him, but Jesus sent him away, saying, "Return to your house, and declare what great things God has done for you." He went his way, proclaiming throughout the whole city what great things Jesus had done for him. Luke 8:26-39

Reflection:

Evil exists. Spiritual warfare is real, but we can keep ourselves safeguarded by seeking Jesus. The devil is strong, but his power is no match for God. When we stay securely within God's strong arms, we can count on him to protect us against spiritual attack. The devil can't stand up to the name of Jesus, so simply proclaiming his name is impenetrable spiritual armor. Seek Jesus by calling on his protection. With Jesus by your side, evil forces don't stand a chance.

Prayer:

Jesus, protect me and my loved ones from evil spirits. Wrap us in your loving arms and shield us from harm. When I call upon your name, drive away any spiritual attacks and fill me with the peace that only you can bring. Never let me get separated from your love or protection. I need you. Amen.

Behold, a man named Jairus came. He was a ruler of the synagogue. He fell down at Jesus' feet and begged him to come into his house, for he had an only born daughter, about twelve years of age, and she was dying. But as he went, the multitudes pressed against him. A woman who had a flow of blood for twelve years, who had spent all her living on physicians and could not be healed by any, came behind him and touched the fringe of his cloak. Immediately the flow of her blood stopped. Jesus said, "Who touched me?" When all denied it, Peter and those with him said, "Master, the multitudes press and jostle you, and you say, 'Who touched me?'" But Jesus said, "Someone did touch me, for I perceived that power has gone out of me." When the woman saw that she was not hidden, she came trembling; and falling down before him declared to him in the presence of all the people the reason why she had touched him, and how she was healed immediately. He said to her, "Daughter, cheer up. Your faith has made you well. Go in peace."

While he still spoke, one from the ruler of the synagogue's house came, saying to him, "Your daughter is dead. Don't trouble the Teacher." But Jesus hearing it, answered him, "Don't be afraid. Only believe, and she will be healed." When he came to the house, he didn't allow anyone to enter in, except Peter, John, James, the father of the child, and her mother. All were weeping and mourning her, but he said, "Don't weep. She isn't dead, but sleeping." They were ridiculing him, knowing that she was dead. But he put them all outside, and taking her by the hand, he called, saying, "Child, arise!" Her spirit returned, and she rose up immediately. He commanded that something be given to her to eat. Luke 8:41-55

Reflection:

Jesus' miracles are historical facts, so it's hard to understand how anyone can simply think he was just a good man, or even a prophet. Raising anyone from the dead is beyond the job description of a prophet, let alone any good man. Jesus' miracles showed us he is God and worthy of our praise and honor. Jesus asked Jairus to have faith, and that's what he's asking of us today. We show him our faith by seeking him with our whole heart.

Prayer:

Lord, I believe in your miracles. I want to experience your majesty in my life and in my heart. Walk with me. Speak to me. Guide me. With you, all things are possible. Thank you for counting me among your children. I love you. Amen.

35

[Jesus] called the twelve together and gave them power and authority over all demons, and to cure diseases. He sent them out to preach God's Kingdom and to heal the sick. He said to them, "Take nothing for your journey—no staffs, nor wallet, nor bread, nor money. Don't have two tunics each. Into whatever house you enter, stay there, and depart from there. As many as don't receive you, when you depart from that city, shake off even the dust from your feet for a testimony against them." They departed and went throughout the villages, preaching the Good News and healing everywhere. Luke 9:1-6

Reflection:

It had been a big deal when the Twelve had left their lives behind to follow Jesus. But they did it to follow the great teacher. However, once Jesus entrusted them with more responsibility, by giving them power and authority, he expected them to go out on their own. This was a game-changer and not what the apostles had signed up for. Being put in this leadership role might have been nerve-racking enough, but without extra clothing, money, or food? They showed extraordinary trust in following those orders. And all their needs were later met, as Jesus knew they would be. Do you have that kind of faith in Jesus? To leave things behind that you don't think you can live without? Do you trust that Jesus will always ensure your needs are met?

Prayer:

Dear Lord, grant me the strong trust that your apostles had. You ask less of me than you did of them, and yet I still falter sometimes. Give me the courage to trust that you will provide all I need. Give me the strength and commitment to follow your will for me without hesitation or question. I ask this in the name of Jesus, the Savior of the world. Amen.

36

The apostles, when they had returned, told [Jesus] what things they had done. He took them and withdrew apart to a desert region of a city called Bethsaida. But the multitudes, perceiving it, followed him. He welcomed them, spoke to them of God's Kingdom, and he cured those who needed healing. The day began to wear away; and the twelve came and said to him, "Send the multitude away, that they may go into the surrounding villages and farms and lodge and get food, for we are here in a deserted place."

But he said to them, "You give them something to eat." They said, "We have no more than five loaves and two fish, unless we should go and buy food for all these people." For they were about five thousand men. He said to his disciples, "Make them sit down in groups of about fifty each." They did so, and made them all sit down. He took the five loaves and the two fish, and looking up to the sky, he blessed them, broke them, and gave them to the disciples to set before the multitude. They ate and were all filled. They gathered up twelve baskets of broken pieces that were left over. Luke 9:10-17

Reflection:

As people became familiar with Jesus, he drew enormous crowds. That popularity is very telling. People were amazed at his miracles. By this time, the apostles had already seen enough to know that Jesus was able to make anything happen. If he said to have five thousand people be seated for a meal, they trusted he would make something happen. And he did. Jesus will never lead us astray. When we listen to his voice and follow his will, we will never fail. If you feel like you have two fish and he's asking you to feed five thousand people, he will make it happen. Open your heart to him. Listen to his will. He will never let you fail.

Prayer:

Jesus, I know that with you, all things are possible. Your miracles prove that. And yet, I still find myself trying to control my life. Speak to me and open my ears to hear. Breathe your will into my heart and help me pay attention to your instructions. Give me the courage to trust that anything you ask of me, you will help me accomplish. Jesus, I believe, but help me in my unbelief. Grant me the courage to be your good and faithful servant. Amen.

37

But [Jesus] warned them and commanded them to tell this to no one, saying, "The Son of Man must suffer many things, and be rejected by the elders, chief priests, and scribes, and be killed, and the third day be raised up." He said to all, "If anyone desires to come after me, let him deny himself, take up his cross, and follow me. For whoever desires to save his life will lose it, but whoever will lose his life for my sake will save it. For what does it profit a man if he gains the whole world, and loses or forfeits his own self? For whoever will be ashamed of me and of my words, of him will the Son of Man be ashamed when he comes in his glory, and the glory of the Father, and of the holy angels." Luke 9:21-26

Reflection:

Even as the picture of who Jesus really was became clearer for the apostles, it's likely they still didn't fully understand what Jesus was predicting when he said these words. When he told them they needed to deny themselves and take up their crosses and that they must lose their lives to save it, those are intimidating words, especially if you don't really understand their meaning. We have the benefit of hindsight, so we understand the meaning of Jesus dying for our salvation and that we must follow him, but it's still intimidating. Do you deny yourself worldly desires? Do you willingly take up the cross? Are you willing to lose your life to save it? We say YES, but do we really? How do you show it?

Prayer:

Dear Lord, I want to follow you, but I also like it to be convenient. Help me to sacrifice myself for you, not just when it's easy. Use me as your servant. Lead me to your will for my life, and give me the faith to trust you'll protect me when the road becomes rough. You knew that you'd be giving up your life for mine, but you didn't back down from the task even though you probably dreaded it. Help me use your example to accept your will for my life, whatever challenges it may bring. Give me the courage to take up my cross and follow you. Amen.

38

About eight days after these sayings, [Jesus] took with him Peter, John, and James, and went up onto the mountain to pray. As he was praying, the appearance of his face was altered, and his clothing became white and dazzling. Behold, two men were talking with him, who were Moses and Elijah, who appeared in glory and spoke of his departure, which he was about to accomplish at Jerusalem.

Now Peter and those who were with him were heavy with sleep, but when they were fully awake, they saw his glory, and the two men who stood with him. As they were parting from him, Peter said to Jesus, "Master, it is good for us to be here. Let's make three tents: one for you, one for Moses, and one for Elijah," not knowing what he said. While he said these things, a cloud came and overshadowed them, and they were afraid as they entered into the cloud. A voice came out of the cloud, saying, "This is my beloved Son. Listen to him!" When the voice came, Jesus was found alone. They were silent, and told no one in those days any of the things which they had seen. Luke 9:28-36

Reflection:

What a majestic glimpse of heavenly splendor these men were given! Yes, it caught them off guard, and they were afraid, but it's really a dream come true to get a peek at the other side. When we seek Jesus, this is what we're striving to attain. The more we give ourselves fully and pursue an intimate relationship with him, the more we're able to understand his communication with us, to see his signs, and hear his answers. If we're fortunate, he gives us amazing glimpses. Seek a deep relationship with Jesus and prepare to be amazed.

Prayer:

Jesus, my heart longs to know you. Help me seek you. Fill my soul with your presence. Teach me to sit patiently in silence and wait for you. Meet me in the stillness. Let me feel your love and hear what you need me to know. Your love completes me. I need you always. Amen.

39

It came to pass, when the days were near that [Jesus] should be taken up, he intently set his face to go to Jerusalem and sent messengers before his face. They went and entered into a village of the Samaritans, so as to prepare for him. They didn't receive him, because he was traveling with his face set toward Jerusalem. When his disciples, James and John, saw this, they said, "Lord, do you want us to command fire to come down from the sky and destroy them, just as Elijah did?" But he turned and rebuked them, "You don't know of what kind of spirit you are. For the Son of Man didn't come to destroy men's lives, but to save them." They went to another village. Luke 9:51-56

Reflection:

Jesus gave us a beautiful life lesson with his example. As his followers, we sometimes struggle with whether we should speak out when we're rebuked. Is this what Jesus asks of us? In this case, he gave the Samaritans the opportunity to host him, but they refused. Rather than argue with them or harm them (as James and John suggested), Jesus moved on. We can use this lesson as we share the Good News within our own calling. When our message is ignored or refused, simply move on and keep sharing the Good News with others. Our job is to plant the seeds. God will make them grow in His timing.

Prayer:

Lord, help me to be a good disciple. Give me courage to speak out on your behalf and share the Good News. Fill my heart with the message you want me to share and give me the right words to say. Give me the strength to continue, even if the message isn't accepted or if I'm reprimanded. There are people waiting to hear your Word. Lead me to them. I ask this in Jesus' name. Amen.

~ *40* ~

Now after these things, the Lord also appointed seventy others, and sent them two by two ahead of him into every city and place where he was about to come. Then he said to them, "The harvest is indeed plentiful, but the laborers are few. Pray therefore to the Lord of the harvest, that he may send out laborers into his harvest. Go your ways. Behold, I send you out as lambs among wolves. Carry no purse, nor wallet, nor sandals. Greet no one on the way." The seventy returned with joy, saying, "Lord, even the demons are subject to us in your name!" Luke 10:1-4, 17

Reflection:

We are the seventy. We are those whom Jesus is sending out and asking to speak out on his behalf. When we go two by two, it's not as intimidating as being out on our own. We can rely on each other for support and guidance. Who's your spiritual partner? Who can help you spread the Good News? Find like-minded people who will walk with you as you venture out into the unknown and sometimes scary territory. The seventy confirm for us that our words and deeds performed in the name of Jesus have immense power. We have the ability to draw people to the Kingdom, and Jesus is asking us to do it. When we seek him, we find ways to do it, even if we're scared and feeling unqualified.

Prayer:

Jesus, help me find ways to lead people to you. Show me what you need from me. Guide me. Put people in my life who can help me accomplish your will for me. Calm my fears and let me trust that I can handle anything you ask of me. Amen.

41

Behold, a certain lawyer stood up and tested [Jesus], saying, "Teacher, what shall I do to inherit eternal life?" He said to him, "What is written in the law? How do you read it?" He answered, "You shall love the Lord your God with all your heart, with all your soul, with all your strength, and with all your mind; and your neighbor as yourself." He said to him, "You have answered correctly. Do this, and you will live." But he, desiring to justify himself, asked Jesus, "Who is my neighbor?"

Jesus answered, "A certain man was going down from Jerusalem to Jericho, and he fell among robbers, who both stripped him and beat him, and departed, leaving him half dead. By chance a certain priest was going down that way. When he saw him, he passed by on the other side. In the same way a Levite also, when he came to the place and saw him, passed by on the other side. But a certain Samaritan, as he traveled, came where he was. When he saw him, he was moved with compassion, came to him, and bound up his wounds, pouring on oil and wine. He set him on his own animal, brought him to an inn, and took care of him. On the next day, when he departed, he took out two denarii, gave them to the host, and said to him, 'Take care of him. Whatever you spend beyond that, I will repay you when I return.' Now which of these three do you think seemed to be a neighbor to him who fell among the robbers?" He said, "He who showed mercy on him." Then Jesus said to him, "Go and do likewise." Luke 10: 25-37

Reflection:

The Good Samaritan story is always a helpful reminder of the importance of loving our neighbor. But let's switch it up a bit and focus instead on Jesus' initial answer... that the way to eternal life is to 'Love the Lord your God with all your heart and with all your soul and with all your strength and with all your mind'. In short, he's saying 'Seek me'. Seeking him means giving one hundred percent of yourself to God. Loving God with everything you have reveals an amazing journey of your heart and soul and opens the door to the Kingdom.

Prayer:

Dear Lord, sometimes I get lulled into thinking that my relationship with you is "good enough" because I fit you into a busy schedule. Help me to never become complacent in my spiritual journey. Show me ways to seek you. I want to hear you speak to me. I long to feel you guiding me. Help me nurture our relationship to the point where my eyes are opened to see glimpses of you and my ears and heart can hear you. I want to seek you with my whole heart, soul, and strength. Help me. Amen.

42

As they went on their way, [Jesus] entered into a certain village, and a certain woman named Martha received him into her house. She had a sister called Mary, who also sat at Jesus' feet and heard his word. But Martha was distracted with much serving, and she came up to him, and said, "Lord, don't you care that my sister left me to serve alone? Ask her therefore to help me." Jesus answered her, "Martha, Martha, you are anxious and troubled about many things, but one thing is needed. Mary has chosen the good part, which will not be taken away from her." Luke 10: 38-42

Reflection:

How many times do we become too distracted with perfection that we lose sight of the things that really matter? Martha represents us when we get that righteous attitude about doing all the right things. But Jesus reminds us that value is only in doing things that matter. He chided Martha for not seeking him as Mary did. Even in our spiritual lives, we need to make the time count. The most valuable time spent building our relationship with God happens within our heart and soul. Anything beyond that is icing on the cake. Let Mary be your example for seeking him. Stop being Martha.

Prayer:

Dear Heavenly Father, remind me to seek you first. Chide me when I take the self-righteous path and squander time that I could be spending with you in my heart. Help me understand the true meaning of seeking you and how it's different than reciting prayers. Let me feel you in my heart. Let me see you before me. Help me allow the words of the prayers and songs to touch my heart and soul in a way that connects me to you. Help me be more like Mary and bask in your presence. I ask this through your son, Jesus Christ. Amen.

~ *43* ~

When [Jesus] finished praying in a certain place, one of his disciples said to him, "Lord, teach us to pray, just as John also taught his disciples." He said to them, "When you pray, say, 'Our Father in heaven, may your name be kept holy. May your Kingdom come. May your will be done on earth, as it is in heaven. Give us day by day our daily bread. Forgive us our sins, for we ourselves also forgive everyone who is indebted to us. Bring us not into temptation, but deliver us from the evil one.'"

He said to them, "Which of you, if you go to a friend at midnight and tell him, 'Friend, lend me three loaves of bread, for a friend of mine has come to me from a journey, and I have nothing to set before him,' and he from within will answer and say, 'Don't bother me. The door is now shut, and my children are with me in bed. I can't get up and give it to you'? I tell you, although he will not rise and give it to him because he is his friend, yet because of his persistence, he will get up and give him as many as he needs. "I tell you, keep asking, and it will be given you. Keep seeking, and you will find. Keep knocking, and it will be opened to you. For everyone who asks receives. He who seeks finds. To him who knocks it will be opened. Which of you fathers, if your son asks for bread, will give him a stone? Or if he asks for a fish, he won't give him a snake instead of a fish, will he? Or if he asks for an egg, he won't give him a scorpion, will he? If you then, being evil, know how to give good gifts to your children, how much more will your heavenly Father give the Holy Spirit to those who ask him?" Luke 11:1-13

Reflection:

Not only is Jesus telling us the words to use when we pray from the beautiful and timeless *Lord's Prayer*, he's telling us once again to seek him. He promises that those who seek will find, even those with shameless audacity who have not nurtured a relationship with him previously. It's never too late to seek him. He's waiting for you. He wants to have an intimate relationship with each of his people. Because he loves us, he gave us free will, which means the choice is ours. He's waiting with open arms for us to turn to him and seek him. Pray *the Lord's Prayer* with full intention. Close your eyes. Hear and feel every word of it in your heart. See yourself in God's presence speaking the words directly to him. If you find yourself skimming over the words, go back and repeat with intention on every word, even if it takes five minutes to complete the thirty-second prayer. He is waiting for you to seek him in this way.

Prayer:

Dear Lord, I know you want me to seek you, and I'd like nothing more than to have a closer relationship with you. Open my heart and lead me closer to you. I love you. Amen.

[Jesus] was casting out a demon, and it was mute. When the demon had gone out, the mute man spoke; and the multitudes marveled. But some of them said, "He casts out demons by Beelzebul (Satan), the prince of the demons." Others, testing him, sought from him a sign from heaven. "He who is not with me is against me. He who doesn't gather with me scatters." Luke 11:14-16, 23

Reflection:

Not everyone chooses Jesus. Even some who witnessed his miracles first-hand didn't believe. We will encounter nonbelievers throughout our lives. Will their doubt cause us to doubt? Will their unbelief shake our faith? These tests of our faith have the potential to tear it apart if we don't have a firm foundation. Shore up the foundation of your faith by seeking Jesus. Whoever is not with him is against him. Stay with him, no matter what doubters say.

Prayer:

Dear Lord, make my faith strong enough to withstand any test. My faith is so strong when I hear from you. Please speak to me, give me signs, show me you're near. Remind me to make seeking you a priority because the closeness of our relationship is my responsibility. You're always there and waiting for me. Never let me leave your side. I ask this in the name of Jesus. Amen.

When the multitudes were gathering together to [Jesus], he began to say, "This is an evil generation. It seeks after a sign. No sign will be given to it but the sign of Jonah the prophet. For even as Jonah became a sign to the Ninevites, so the Son of Man will also be to this generation. Luke 11:29-30

Reflection:

When we seek him, Jesus answers. God speaks to us. He does give us signs, and we may miss them if we're not paying attention. Our personal messages from God may not be as frequent or as bold as we might like them to be. But we have to appreciate the signs we get and use them to help expand his Kingdom. We can't expect constant signs so that we keep believing. Keep seeking and God will reward it. Any relationship that's nurtured becomes naturally stronger than one that's neglected. So, keeping your faith strong comes through nurturing your relationship with Jesus – that is, seeking him.

Prayer:

Lord, I love getting signs from you. I long for them and I'm always craving more. They make me feel safe, loved, and awestruck. They let me know you're near. You sent your son as the biggest sign of all, and when my faith starts to weaken, I can use Jesus to boost me back up again. But I selfishly treasure your personal signs to me. Show me how to seek you so I can find you more often. I love you always. Amen.

No one, when he has lit a lamp, puts it in a cellar or under a basket, but on a stand, that those who come in may see the light. The lamp of the body is the eye. Therefore when your eye is good, your whole body is also full of light; but when it is evil, your body also is full of darkness. Therefore see whether the light that is in you isn't darkness. If therefore your whole body is full of light, having no part dark, it will be wholly full of light, as when the lamp with its bright shining gives you light. Luke 11:33-36

Reflection:

Jesus is the light. He shines bright for all to see, and his light cannot be dimmed. When we are filled with Jesus, we are full of light. When we are full of Jesus, how do we shine that light upon others? How do people see Jesus through us? Do people look at us and see the amazing wonder of God, or do they see darkness from within? Do they see a gossip, a liar, a hypocrite? Or do they see love, kindness, and compassion? We keep God's light shining within us by keeping him close. Our light shines brightest when we seek him with all our hearts.

Prayer:

Dear Heavenly Father, I know that when I'm closest to you, I'm happy and fulfilled. You bring me peace and joy that I pray shines a light as an example for others around me. I want to show people your light that fills me. Help me sweep the darkness away by relinquishing those selfish and ugly parts that I hide from people and that separate me from you. Give me the strength and courage to shine brightly as your disciple. I ask this through your Son, Jesus Christ. Amen.

Now as [Jesus] spoke, a certain Pharisee asked him to dine with him. He went in and sat at the table. When the Pharisee saw it, he marveled that he had not first washed himself before dinner. The Lord said to him, "Now you Pharisees cleanse the outside of the cup and of the platter, but your inward part is full of extortion and wickedness. You foolish ones, didn't he who made the outside make the inside also? But give for gifts to the needy those things which are within, and behold, all things will be clean to you. But woe to you Pharisees! For you tithe mint and rue and every herb, but you bypass justice and God's love. You ought to have done these, and not to have left the other undone. Woe to you Pharisees! For you love the best seats in the synagogues and the greetings in the marketplaces. Woe to you, scribes and Pharisees, hypocrites! For you are like hidden graves, and the men who walk over them don't know it." One of the lawyers answered him, "Teacher, in saying this you insult us also."

He said, "Woe to you lawyers also! For you load men with burdens that are difficult to carry, and you yourselves won't even lift one finger to help carry those burdens. Woe to you! For you build the tombs of the prophets, and your fathers killed them. So you testify and consent to the works of your fathers. For they killed them, and you build their tombs. Therefore also the wisdom of God said, 'I will send to them prophets and apostles; and some of them they will kill and persecute, that the blood of all the prophets, which was shed from the foundation of the world, may be required of this generation, from the blood of Abel to the blood of Zachariah, who perished between the altar and the sanctuary.' Yes, I tell you, it will be required of this generation. Woe to you lawyers! For you took away the key of knowledge. You didn't enter in yourselves, and those who were entering in, you hindered." As he said these things to them, the scribes and the Pharisees began to be terribly angry, and to draw many things out of him, lying in wait for him, and seeking to catch him in something he might say, that they might accuse him. Luke 11:37-46, 53-54

Reflection:

Jesus called the hypocritical Pharisees out, and he does the same to us when we put focus on superficial exterior appearances and neglect the condition of what's inside us. When you take an objective look in the mirror, what do you see? Do you see someone doing "good" things for the recognition it might bring? Do you see someone helping others because it benefits them? Or do you see a person who's seeking Jesus and living according to God's ways? How do your actions and intentions stack up?

Prayer:

Jesus, you see through me and even see me better than I see myself. Please help me keep pure motives. Remind me to perform kind and generous acts out of the public eye and stop me when I start judging others while my own heart is with sin. Lord, cleanse me of the self-centered and judgmental me. Help me seek you and live righteously instead. I pray in your holy name. Amen.

48

I tell you, my friends, don't be afraid of those who kill the body, and after that have no more that they can do. But I will warn you whom you should fear. Fear him who after he has killed, has power to cast into [hell]. Yes, I tell you, fear him. Aren't five sparrows sold for two assaria coins? Not one of them is forgotten by God. But the very hairs of your head are all counted. Therefore don't be afraid. You are of more value than many sparrows.

I tell you, everyone who confesses me before men, the Son of Man will also confess before the angels of God; but he who denies me in the presence of men will be denied in the presence of God's angels. Everyone who speaks a word against the Son of Man will be forgiven, but those who blaspheme against the Holy Spirit will not be forgiven. When they bring you before the synagogues, the rulers, and the authorities, don't be anxious how or what you will answer or what you will say; for the Holy Spirit will teach you in that same hour what you must say. Luke 12:4-12

Reflection:

Jesus reminds us that God's love for each of us is tremendous (he knows every hair on our heads!), but we also have a responsibility to know and acknowledge him. When we seek Jesus, the Holy Spirit provides discernment. Pray for the words to use both to defend and proclaim your faith, and the Holy Spirit will always provide them.

Prayer:

Dear Heavenly Father, I rely on the power of the Holy Spirit to fill me with the words to reach your people and to respond to nonbelievers. On my own, I am nothing. With your help, I can accomplish your will for me. Lead me and I will follow. I pray in Jesus' name. Amen.

49

One of the multitude said to [Jesus], "Teacher, tell my brother to divide the inheritance with me." But he said to him, "Man, who made me a judge or an arbitrator over you?" He said to them, "Beware! Keep yourselves from covetousness, for a man's life doesn't consist of the abundance of the things which he possesses."

He spoke a parable to them, saying, "The ground of a certain rich man produced abundantly. He reasoned within himself, saying, 'What will I do, because I don't have room to store my crops?' He said, 'This is what I will do. I will pull down my barns, build bigger ones, and there I will store all my grain and my goods. I will tell my soul, "Soul, you have many goods laid up for many years. Take your ease, eat, drink, and be merry."' But God said to him, 'You foolish one, tonight your soul is required of you. The things which you have prepared—whose will they be?' So is he who lays up treasure for himself, and is not rich toward God."
Luke 12:13-21

Reflection:

Money is a powerful and sneaky idol. It's one thing to be prudent with money; it's another thing to let money take control of you and turn to greed. Take a moment for serious self-reflection. Do you seek money to amass things or stockpile? Does money come between relationships in your life? Have you let money control you from paycheck to paycheck? Take heed. Life does not exist in abundance of possessions. Life exists when you seek Jesus.

Prayer:

Dear Lord, I thank you for the blessings you've given me in my life. My job, my home, my family. We have everything we need... clothing, food, shelter, each other, and you. I know you will give us our daily bread. Help me not worry about having enough. Help me trust that you will provide as long as I'm prudent. Give me the strength to stand up to the idol of money and fight off the urge to be greedy. I ask this in the name of Jesus Christ, my Redeemer. Amen.

50

[Jesus] said to his disciples, "Therefore I tell you, don't be anxious for your life, what you will eat, nor yet for your body, what you will wear. Life is more than food, and the body is more than clothing. Consider the ravens: they don't sow, they don't reap, they have no warehouse or barn, and God feeds them. How much more valuable are you than birds! Which of you by being anxious can add a cubit to his height? If then you aren't able to do even the least things, why are you anxious about the rest? Consider the lilies, how they grow. They don't toil, neither do they spin; yet I tell you, even Solomon in all his glory was not arrayed like one of these. But if this is how God clothes the grass in the field, which today exists and tomorrow is cast into the oven, how much more will he clothe you, O you of little faith? Don't seek what you will eat or what you will drink; neither be anxious. For the nations of the world seek after all of these things, but your Father knows that you need these things. But seek God's Kingdom, and all these things will be added to you. Don't be afraid, little flock, for it is your Father's good pleasure to give you the Kingdom. Sell what you have and give gifts to the needy. Make for yourselves purses which don't grow old, a treasure in the heavens that doesn't fail, where no thief approaches and no moth destroys. For where your treasure is, there will your heart be also." Luke 12:22-34

Reflection:

What a beautiful gift Jesus gave to the worriers with this description of God's amazing love and care for us. Indeed, if he ensures the birds have the food they need and dresses wildflowers in amazing splendor, how could we not trust that he will provide for us? Once again, he's asking us to seek him. Seek God's Kingdom, and all these things will be given to you as well. God wants to provide for all your needs. But he also wants you to know him. Turn your worry over to him and seek him.

Prayer:

Lord, I see the amazing way you take care of all your creation. The birds don't stockpile food. They trust they will always have enough. Help me turn over my worry to you and live freely, like a bird. Let me trust in your Word. Please reveal yourself to me when I seek you. Tell me what I need to hear. Guide me. Teach me. Help me turn my worry into obedience. Thank you for loving me beyond comprehension. In Jesus' name, I pray. Amen.

51

Let your waist be dressed and your lamps burning. Be like men watching for their lord when he returns from the wedding feast, that when he comes and knocks, they may immediately open to him. Blessed are those servants whom the lord will find watching when he comes. Most certainly I tell you that he will dress himself, make them recline, and will come and serve them. They will be blessed if he comes in the second or third watch and finds them so. But know this, that if the master of the house had known in what hour the thief was coming, he would have watched and not allowed his house to be broken into. Therefore be ready also, for the Son of Man is coming in an hour that you don't expect him. Luke 12:35-40

Reflection:

We all live through various seasons in life, including our spiritual life. Maybe a tragedy alienated us from God, or maybe it drew us closer. But when we seek him, we're dressed and have our lamps burning. We don't have to worry so much about when he's coming, because we've prepared as much as possible, and we stay ready while waiting. Seeking is about nurturing an ongoing relationship. It's not about waiting until company arrives before lighting the lamp and jumping into action. Seeking Jesus keeps you dressed and ready for service, with your lamp burning brightly.

Prayer:

Dear Heavenly Father, I long to be your good servant. Prepare me to do your will. Help me keep my lamp shining brightly for you. Forgive me when I get lazy and don't offer you the best of me. I want to be of service to you during this life and to be ready when my time here is over. I can only accomplish it through your love and grace. Thank you for loving a sinner like me. Amen.

I came to throw fire on the earth. I wish it were already kindled. But I have a baptism to be baptized with, and how distressed I am until it is accomplished! Do you think that I have come to give peace in the earth? I tell you, no, but rather division. For from now on, there will be five in one house divided, three against two, and two against three. They will be divided, father against son, and son against father; mother against daughter, and daughter against her mother; mother-in-law against her daughter-in-law, and daughter-in-law against her mother-in-law. Luke 12:49-53

Reflection:

Jesus promised that following him brings amazing rewards, but he never promised it would be easy. We need to take a stand to defend his way, and sometimes that's going to oppose beliefs of those we love. Are you strong enough to keep standing for Christ amid the opposition? Seek his counsel. Seek his guidance. Pray for your nonbelieving family or friends.

Prayer:

Jesus, you made the ultimate sacrifice for me, and I know the way to the Father is not always easy. Please stand beside me when I have to make choices for you that I know will create division among my family or friends. I choose you above all things. Give me the strength to always choose you. Please send the Holy Spirit to breathe your word into the hearts and souls of my nonbelieving loved ones. Call their names and let them feel your love. I ask all this in your holy name. Amen.

Now there were some present at the same time who told [Jesus] about the Galileans whose blood Pilate had mixed with their sacrifices. Jesus answered them, "Do you think that these Galileans were worse sinners than all the other Galileans, because they suffered such things? I tell you, no, but unless you repent, you will all perish in the same way. Or those eighteen on whom the tower in Siloam fell and killed them—do you think that they were worse offenders than all the men who dwell in Jerusalem? I tell you, no, but, unless you repent, you will all perish in the same way."

He spoke this parable. "A certain man had a fig tree planted in his vineyard, and he came seeking fruit on it and found none. He said to the vine dresser, 'Behold, these three years I have come looking for fruit on this fig tree, and found none. Cut it down! Why does it waste the soil?' He answered, 'Lord, leave it alone this year also, until I dig around it and fertilize it. If it bears fruit, fine; but if not, after that, you can cut it down.'" Luke 13:1-9

Reflection:

Jesus gives us two key lessons in this reading. First, he assures us that the suffering we face in life isn't a result of the amount of our sin. Second, our eternal fate is based on whether or not we turn to Christ and repent of our sins. God gives us ample opportunity to turn to him. He waits for us to tend and fertilize the tree of our faith in order to bear fruit. But at some point, time runs out. The choice is ours all along. When we seek Jesus, we choose him. And when we choose him, we become more like him and bear good fruit.

Prayer:

Dear Lord, I regret all my sins that have separated me from you. Please forgive me and help me walk forward in your light always. I choose you through all the difficulties of life. I choose you when my faith gets weak. Through your grace and strength, I can bear fruit. Use me to shine your light for others. Thank you for loving me even though I'm not worthy. I remain your humble servant in the name of Jesus Christ, my Savior. Amen.

54

[Jesus] was teaching in one of the synagogues on the Sabbath day. Behold, there was a woman who had a spirit of infirmity eighteen years. She was bent over and could in no way straighten herself up. When Jesus saw her, he called her and said to her, "Woman, you are freed from your infirmity." He laid his hands on her, and immediately she stood up straight and glorified God. The ruler of the synagogue, being indignant because Jesus had healed on the Sabbath, said to the multitude, "There are six days in which men ought to work. Therefore come on those days and be healed, and not on the Sabbath day!"

Therefore the Lord answered him, "You hypocrites! Doesn't each one of you free his ox or his donkey from the stall on the Sabbath and lead him away to water? Ought not this woman, being a daughter of Abraham whom Satan had bound eighteen long years, be freed from this bondage on the Sabbath day?" As he said these things, all his adversaries were disappointed; and all the multitude rejoiced for all the glorious things that were done by him. Luke 13:10-17

Reflection:

The hypocritical church leaders of the time called Jesus out on his good works, although they did similar things but without righteous reason. Jesus reminds us that good work on God's behalf is never wrong. Don't get so caught up in rules that you lose track of Christ's message. Let those who cast accusations heed Jesus' words to the synagogue leader.

Prayer:

Dear Heavenly Father, please help me keep my heart pure. Remind me to do good works for righteous reasons and show me when I'm being hypocritical. Remind me of my own transgressions and failures to follow your will. When I feel myself judging someone's sin, give me the grace to turn it over to you. Help me stay humble and loving, just as Jesus did. Amen.

~ 55 ~

[Jesus] said, "What is God's Kingdom like? To what shall I com-pare it? It is like a grain of mustard seed which a man took and put in his own garden. It grew and became a large tree, and the birds of the sky live in its branches." Luke 13:18-19

Reflection:

The mustard seed parable is a short and beautiful example of the Kingdom of God and how we can grow our tiny, doubtful faith into a beautiful, life-giving gift for the glory of the Kingdom. When we tend to the tiny seed, giving it the food, water, sunshine, weeding, and care that it needs, it keeps growing bigger. Finally, it supports life for other creatures. This is the goal of seeking God. Seeking God nurtures our tiny speck of faith into a life-giving gift for the world that leads to God's Kingdom. It's truly magnificent.

Prayer:

Dear Lord, sometimes my faith feels like a tiny speck. Let me feel your presence when my faith is shaken. Please reveal yourself to me and give me signs that you're with me. Give me the strength to keep seeking you during doubtful times. I long to have a huge, beautiful faith, and I know it's possible when I seek you. Help me nurture my faith to use for your glory. I ask this in the glorious name of Jesus Christ. Amen.

56

[Jesus] went on his way through cities and villages, teaching, and traveling on to Jerusalem. One said to him, "Lord, are they few who are saved?"

He said to them, "Strive to enter in by the narrow door, for many, I tell you, will seek to enter in and will not be able. When once the master of the house has risen up and has shut the door, and you begin to stand outside and to knock at the door, saying, 'Lord, Lord, open to us!' then he will answer and tell you, 'I don't know you or where you come from.' Then you will begin to say, 'We ate and drank in your presence, and you taught in our streets.' He will say, 'I tell you, I don't know where you come from. Depart from me, all you workers of iniquity (sinners).'" Luke 13:22-27

Reflection:

This story that Jesus told is one of the most sobering messages of the Bible. He said the door (to the Kingdom) is narrow. But don't give up hope, because it's open to all who seek him. This reading is our reminder that hollow words and actions, however good-intentioned they are, don't fool God. What he expects from us is to *know* us—from the heart. Superficial niceties don't work. Seek him with your heart and soul, and the door will be wide open.

Prayer:

Dear Heavenly Father, I fear not being able to enter into eternity with you. Let this stark reminder of the "narrow door" give me the motivation to put you first in my life, to seek you before life itself. When I enter the gates, I pray you recognize me as your good and faithful servant. I pray the Holy Spirit will breathe your Word into my loved ones so they will turn to you, too. Help me shine your light for them and for all who cross my path. I ask this in Jesus' name. Amen.

57

On that same day, some Pharisees came, saying to [Jesus], "Get out of here and go away, for Herod wants to kill you." He said to them, "Go and tell that fox, 'Behold, I cast out demons and perform cures today and tomorrow, and the third day I complete my mission. Nevertheless I must go on my way today and tomorrow and the next day, for it can't be that a prophet would perish outside of Jerusalem.'

Jerusalem, Jerusalem, you who kills the prophets and stones those who are sent to her! How often I wanted to gather your children together, like a hen gathers her own brood under her wings, and you refused! Behold, your house is left to you desolate. I tell you, you will not see me until you say, 'Blessed is he who comes in the name of the Lord!'" Luke 13:31-35

Reflection:

Jesus longs to draw us to him. It pains him when we're not willing. We might wonder why he lets us wander away and doesn't pull us back. He shows his love by granting us free will and leaving our life choices up to us. But it's through our own free will that we must turn to him. We can use his example in this verse to keep pressing on today, tomorrow, and the next day as we use our lives to shine his light.

Prayer:

Jesus, my life goes off track when I turn from you. When I make decisions according to my own wishes without consideration of your will, it doesn't work out well. Please keep calling me back when I stray. Help me be a living example for others. Let me exude the joy that living life for you brings. Help me keep pressing on by using your example. I love you forever. Amen.

[Jesus] also said to the one who had invited him, "When you make a dinner or a supper, don't call your friends, nor your brothers, nor your kinsmen, nor rich neighbors, or perhaps they might also return the favor, and pay you back. But when you make a feast, ask the poor, the maimed, the lame, or the blind; and you will be blessed, because they don't have the resources to repay you. For you will be repaid in the resurrection of the righteous." Luke 14:12-14

Reflection:

It's easiest and most comfortable for us to associate with our friends and family. Jesus challenges us to extend beyond that comfort zone and instead reach out to the less fortunate. To help those in need who can't otherwise repay. How can you find ways to apply this request to your life?

Prayer:

Dear Heavenly Father, through your love and kindness, I have so many blessings in my life. Help me find ways to share with those who are less fortunate and aren't able to repay. Put people in my path or lead me to seek them out. Stand by my side as I step out of my comfort zone to help your people in need. I ask this in the name of your Son, Jesus Christ. Amen.

[A man at the dinner table with Jesus said, "Blessed is he who will feast in God's Kingdom!"]

But [Jesus} said to him, "A certain man made a great supper, and he invited many people. He sent out his servant at supper time to tell those who were invited, 'Come, for everything is ready now.' They all as one began to make excuses. The first said to him, 'I have bought a field, and I must go and see it. Please have me excused.' Another said, 'I have bought five yoke of oxen, and I must go try them out. Please have me excused.' Another said, 'I have married a wife, and therefore I can't come.' That servant came, and told his lord these things. Then the master of the house, being angry, said to his servant, 'Go out quickly into the streets and lanes of the city, and bring in the poor, maimed, blind, and lame.' The servant said, 'Lord, it is done as you commanded, and there is still room.' The lord said to the servant, 'Go out into the highways and hedges, and compel them to come in, that my house may be filled.'" Luke 14:16-23

Reflection:

We all have an open invitation to the incredible banquet of the Lord. He gives us free will to either join him or make excuses as to why we won't. What choice are you making? Do you cherish the opportunity to spend time with the Lord, or find all the reasons why you can't or won't? Do you keep thinking you'll get to Jesus tomorrow or some other day? Once you're less busy and life settles down a bit? We have an invitation awaiting us daily. Every day you decline it is a lost opportunity to lead the life you're called to live.

<u>Prayer:</u>

Dear Lord, I know you love me and you're awaiting my arrival at your banquet. Sometimes I fall short and make excuses why I can't come, but you know that there are no valid excuses. When I become too self-absorbed or decide I can handle life without your guidance, please pull me back to the right path. I want to enjoy the banquet you prepared for your people. I say YES to your invitation. I love you. Amen.

60

Now great multitudes were going with [Jesus]. He turned and said to them, "If anyone comes to me, and doesn't disregard his own father, mother, wife, children, brothers, and sisters, yes, and his own life also, he can't be my disciple. Whoever doesn't bear his own cross and come after me, can't be my disciple. For which of you, desiring to build a tower, doesn't first sit down and count the cost, to see if he has enough to complete it? Or perhaps, when he has laid a foundation and isn't able to finish, everyone who sees begins to mock him, saying, 'This man began to build and wasn't able to finish.' Or what king, as he goes to encounter another king in war, will not sit down first and consider whether he is able with ten thousand to meet him who comes against him with twenty thousand? Or else, while the other is yet a great way off, he sends an envoy and asks for conditions of peace. So therefore, whoever of you who doesn't renounce all that he has, he can't be my disciple. Luke 14:25-33

Reflection:

Following Jesus isn't for the faint of heart! Thankfully, he provides everything we need to follow him if we truly desire to do so. If we really think of giving up our lives for him or turning against our family for him, are those prices we'd be willing to pay? Luckily, most of us won't face life or death decisions, but we might certainly have to choose Jesus over the objections or ridicule of family or friends. It takes strength and courage to follow him. Seek him, and he will provide all the strength and courage you need when any opposition comes.

Prayer:

Dear Holy Lord, you provide me with everything I need. I thank you that I live in a society that won't harm me for following you. Bless and protect people in the world who face persecution for their faith in you. Give me the strength and courage to stand up to any opposition I face for being a Christian. With you by my side, I can handle any challenges. I choose you. Help me stay the course. I ask this in the name of Jesus Christ, Savior of the world. Amen.

[Jesus] told them this parable: "Which of you men, if you had one hundred sheep and lost one of them, wouldn't leave the ninety-nine in the wilderness and go after the one that was lost, until he found it? When he has found it, he carries it on his shoulders, rejoicing. When he comes home, he calls together his friends and his neighbors, saying to them, 'Rejoice with me, for I have found my sheep which was lost!' I tell you that even so there will be more joy in heaven over one sinner who repents, than over ninety-nine righteous people who need no repentance." Luke 15:3-7

Reflection:

Our Father longs to have all his people at his side. Here, he gives two critical messages for us, both when we're the obedient sheep and when we're the lost sheep, because it's likely we'll relate to each of these roles at different points in our lives. This reading addresses the first case of the wandering sheep: the one who walked away. When we fall away from God, he doesn't give up on us. He wants us to come back so badly that he leaves the others to pursue us. He rejoices when we turn to him, and he carries us back to the flock with great joy. God will always welcome us with joy and open arms. We never have to fear turning back to him.

Prayer:

Dear Father in Heaven, thank you for your endless love, even when I'm undeserving. How beautiful it is that you rejoice when your lost sheep are found. Keep me by your side. I know when I stay near, you provide me with all I need. You never forsake your people when we turn to you. Keep searching for those who are currently lost and never give up on me when I go astray. I ask this in the name of Jesus Christ. Amen.

62

But he was angry and would not go in. Therefore his father came out and begged him. But he answered his father, "Behold, these many years I have served you, and I never disobeyed a commandment of yours, but you never gave me a goat, that I might celebrate with my friends. But when this your son came, who has devoured your living with prostitutes, you killed the fattened calf for him." He said to him, "Son, you are always with me, and all that is mine is yours. But it was appropriate to celebrate and be glad, for this, your brother, was dead, and is alive again. He was lost, and is found." Luke 15:28-32

Reflection:

The ending of the Parable of the Prodigal Son (or Lost Son) is where the older son reprimands his father for what he perceives as unfair treatment. This is the flip side of the parable, when we may relate to the older son's indignation when his squandering brother is rewarded with a celebration. If you ever feel God hasn't "rewarded" you enough for your good works or hard efforts for the Kingdom, remind yourself of this: Those who stay with the Father are *always* rewarded with his constant love and everything they could possibly need. What more could we ask for? Why begrudge a brother whose return home delights the father? Join the celebration instead!

Prayer:

Lord, you give me everything I need. When I perceive that you reward others more than I'm rewarded, or when the Prodigal Son seems to be rewarded for bad behavior, remind me that I have no room to complain. You are there for me every step of the way. Help me focus on my relationship with you and not judge anyone else's relationship with you. You love all your people, and as long as I'm loved, there is nothing more I need. I love you. Amen.

He who is faithful in a very little is faithful also in much. He who is dishonest in a very little is also dishonest in much. If therefore you have not been faithful in the unrighteous mammon (money), who will commit to your trust the true riches? If you have not been faithful in that which is another's, who will give you that which is your own? No servant can serve two masters, for either he will hate the one and love the other; or else he will hold to one and despise the other. You aren't able to serve God and [money]. Luke 16:10-13

Reflection:

Jesus makes it very clear: You cannot serve both God and money. Most of us would readily say, "I choose God." If you think you have chosen God, let's take a closer look. Use this opportunity to search your heart and see if that's really the case. Are you trying to serve both God and money? When we genuinely seek Jesus, we stop seeking money as a goal and use the money we have to do good for those in need. After your self-assessment, do you need to realign your priorities?

Prayer:

Dear Heavenly Father, you are my one true God. Help me forsake all the trappings of the world and worship you alone. Help me use money to further your Kingdom and help the needy, as well as provide for my family's needs. Take away my envy of houses that are bigger than mine, cars that have prestigious insignias, and all the glitter of a "Hollywood" lifestyle. I have you, and you provide everything I need, and that is enough. Your riches are worth more than all the gold in the world. Please keep me grounded in your love. I pray in Jesus' name. Amen.

Everyone who divorces his wife and marries another commits adultery. He who marries one who is divorced from a husband commits adultery. Luke 16:18

Reflection:

Today's divorce rate proves that we've lost sight of God's will on marriage. In our me-me-me society, divorce and remarriage are commonplace. Today's reading reminds us that God designed marriage to be for keeps. Wherever we are in our journey of marriage or singlehood, today is the day to decide that marriage is for keeps. That mindset makes us more discerning of who a good spouse would be and also prevents harm to children from seeing a parade of suitors come and go in their lives. Each of us decides the conditions under which a marriage needs to be dissolved, and there are definitely valid reasons. Jesus specifically allowed it in the case of sexual immorality in Matthew 5:32. But when we look at marriage through God's eyes while we're dating, we make decisions that ensure a lifelong commitment to marriage is possible.

Prayer:

Dear Lord, forgive me for the mistakes I've made while dating and/or married. Help me to move forward with your will in my heart. Guide my decisions to ensure a lifelong marriage. May I be an example for others of what being a good partner in a godly marriage looks like. Bless my current (or future) spouse and remind me that when I keep you in the forefront, I will make decisions that lead to my happiness as well as yours. Thank you for the blessing of marriage. May I use it wisely and according to your will. Amen.

~ *65* ~

"Now there was a certain rich man, and he was clothed in purple and fine linen, living in luxury every day. A certain beggar, named Lazarus, was taken to his gate, full of sores, and desiring to be fed with the crumbs that fell from the rich man's table. Yes, even the dogs came and licked his sores. The beggar died, and he was carried away by the angels to Abraham's bosom. The rich man also died and was buried. In Hades, he lifted up his eyes, being in torment, and saw Abraham far off, and Lazarus at his bosom. He cried and said, 'Father Abraham, have mercy on me, and send Lazarus, that he may dip the tip of his finger in water and cool my tongue! For I am in anguish in this flame.'

"But Abraham said, 'Son, remember that you, in your lifetime, received your good things, and Lazarus, in the same way, bad things. But here he is now comforted and you are in anguish. Besides all this, between us and you there is a great gulf fixed, that those who want to pass from here to you are not able, and that no one may cross over from there to us.'

"He said, 'I ask you therefore, father, that you would send him to my father's house—for I have five brothers—that he may testify to them, so they won't also come into this place of torment.' "But Abraham said to him, 'They have Moses and the prophets. Let them listen to them.' "He said, 'No, father Abraham, but if one goes to them from the dead, they will repent.' "He said to him, 'If they don't listen to Moses and the prophets, neither will they be persuaded if one rises from the dead.'" Luke 16:19-31

Reflection:

Jesus cautions us in many ways that the choices we make on earth will have lasting impact. But these verses also highlight a different truth. As believers, we sometimes think that if people just see enough signs, they will come to believe. But if Jesus' rising from the dead isn't enough evidence, there's little we can say to change their minds, because the choice happens in the heart. However, there are at least two things we can do to help nonbelievers. First, we can pray that they open their minds and hearts to Jesus. Second, we can keep shining God's light and spreading his Word through our own words and actions.

Prayer:

Lord, have mercy on nonbelievers. Please send the Holy Spirit to breathe truth into their hearts. Call them by name loudly so they will hear your voice. Help me live my life as an example of your glory for nonbelievers. Give me the words to say when they have questions or concerns. Let me shine your light on them by how I live my life. Lord, show me how to plant seeds of faith. I ask this in Jesus' name. Amen.

He said to the disciples, "It is impossible that no occasions of stumbling should come, but woe to him through whom they come! It would be better for him if a millstone were hung around his neck, and he were thrown into the sea, rather than that he should cause one of these little ones to stumble." Luke 17:1-2

Reflection:

Jesus gave a stern and grave warning here. Are we the hands and feet and voice of God, or are we the reason why other people stumble? Jesus cautions us to watch ourselves. Woe to those who cause others to stumble in their journey. Does your jealousy, greed, or gossiping cause others to stumble? Do your words and actions build people up or tear them down?

Prayer:

Dear Lord, let me be a person who lifts others up and helps them along in their Christian journey. Sometimes my insecurities and selfishness cause me to tear others down, even if it's only in my mind. I lay my failings down at your feet. Please forgive me. Take away my hurtful thoughts and actions and help me be the one who raises people up and shines your light to the world. I can do all things with your help. Amen.

~ *67* ~

Be careful. If your brother sins against you, rebuke him. If he repents, forgive him. If he sins against you seven times in the day, and seven times returns, saying, "I repent," you shall forgive him."
Luke 17:3-4

Reflection:

Forgiving those who've wronged us is one of the most difficult things to do. Many times, we hear it said that the "Christian" thing to do is to forgive someone, but we leave out important aspects of what Jesus requires of us. First, he says to rebuke those who sin against us. We aren't called to be doormats. When someone hurts or disappoints us, we should speak up and speak out for ourselves. Then, *if they repent*, forgive them. We aren't obligated to forgive someone who isn't sorry for how they've mistreated us, but letting it go from our heart is ultimately a life-giving gift to ourselves, just as Jesus forgave those who were torturing him. However, when someone genuinely repents for hurting us, we're called to forgive them, as many times as they truly repent. How many times do we keep failing and want to be forgiven? As Jesus forgives us when we repent, he expects us to do the same for others.

Prayer:

Dear Lord, give me a forgiving heart. Let me learn from your example and forgive those who hurt me, even when it feels impossible. Help me discern when it's time to walk away from people in my life. Guide me to people who build me up instead of tear me down, and help me be a person who builds other people up. Jesus, you gave me the ultimate example of forgiveness. Please help me follow your lead. Amen.

68

As [Jesus] was on his way to Jerusalem, he was passing along the borders of Samaria and Galilee. As he entered into a certain village, ten men who were lepers met him, who stood at a distance. They lifted up their voices, saying, "Jesus, Master, have mercy on us!"

When he saw them, he said to them, "Go and show yourselves to the priests." As they went, they were cleansed. One of them, when he saw that he was healed, turned back, glorifying God with a loud voice. He fell on his face at Jesus' feet, giving him thanks; and he was a Samaritan. Jesus answered, "Weren't the ten cleansed? But where are the nine? Were there none found who returned to give glory to God, except this foreigner?" Then he said to him, "Get up, and go your way. Your faith has healed you." Luke 17:11-19

Reflection:

It seems unfathomable that only one out of ten cured lepers returned to thank Jesus and praise God for their healing. But we can often see the hand of God at work in our own lives. Are we always grateful? Do we share the good works with others and praise him, or do we simply accept the gift and move on to the next thing? Have we stopped appreciating God's gifts? How does it feel when someone pushes our gift aside?

Prayer:

Dear Heavenly Father, thank you for the wonderful and mighty ways you've worked miracles in my life. They always fill my heart with such joy and appreciation, but I might not always give you the praise and thanks you deserve. Give me an appreciative heart. Help me see my selfish ways and learn to care more about you and others than for myself. Forgive me for taking you for granted. I pray I can be the loving and appreciative child you deserve. I ask this in Jesus' name. Amen.

69

[Jesus] said to the disciples, "The days will come when you will desire to see one of the days of the Son of Man, and you will not see it. They will tell you, 'Look, here!' or 'Look, there!' Don't go away or follow after them, for as the lightning, when it flashes out of one part under the sky, shines to another part under the sky, so will the Son of Man be in his day. But first, he must suffer many things and be rejected by this generation. As it was in the days of Noah, even so it will also be in the days of the Son of Man. They ate, they drank, they married, and they were given in marriage until the day that Noah entered into the ship, and the flood came and destroyed them all. Likewise, even as it was in the days of Lot: they ate, they drank, they bought, they sold, they planted, they built; but in the day that Lot went out from Sodom, it rained fire and sulfur from the sky and destroyed them all. It will be the same way in the day that the Son of Man is revealed." Luke 17:22-30

Reflection:

When we seek Jesus, our hearts and souls are always prepared for the day of his return. If we keep pushing off a commitment to God, thinking there will always be time later, we may run out of time. Besides, why put off the richest and most fulfilling experience we can possibly have on earth, which only happens when we walk alongside Jesus? Heed his warning and seek him.

Prayer:

Dear God, I long to see you someday in all your glory. I'm a sinner, and it's through my repentance and your forgiveness and grace that I may be accepted into your heavenly Kingdom. Forgive me and my loved ones when we've fallen out of line with your will. Call us to your side and never let us go. Help us to prepare our hearts and souls for your return. I pray this in the holy name of Jesus. Amen.

70

[Jesus] also spoke a parable to them that they must always pray and not give up, saying, "There was a judge in a certain city who didn't fear God and didn't respect man. A widow was in that city, and she often came to him, saying, 'Defend me from my adversary!' He wouldn't for a while; but afterward he said to himself, 'Though I neither fear God nor respect man, yet because this widow bothers me, I will defend her, or else she will wear me out by her continual coming.'"

The Lord said, "Listen to what the unrighteous judge says. Won't God avenge his chosen ones who are crying out to him day and night, and yet he exercises patience with them? I tell you that he will avenge them quickly. Nevertheless, when the Son of Man comes, will he find faith on the earth?" Luke 18:1-8

Reflection:

God is asking us to seek him and to cry out for him day and night. He wants to be more than a passing thought once a day or once a week. Those who seek him relentlessly are following his will. He's asking us to lay our problems at his feet, to come to him for comfort, and trust that he will help us through our difficulties. Cry out to him. See yourself at his feet. Feel his mercy and comfort. Seek him. You will see his works and hear him when he reveals himself to you.

Prayer:

Dear Heavenly Father, I relinquish my problems into your hands. Give me strength to wait for the resolution and not be discouraged. Send your Holy Spirit to stay by my side while I wait for answers. Give me patience and hope. Remind me that all things are possible through you. You know what I need better than I know it myself. Help me accept your will for my struggles and give up my own desires. I need you and know you won't forsake me. I ask this through your Son, Jesus Christ. Amen.

[Jesus] also spoke this parable to certain people who were convinced of their own righteousness, and who despised all others: "Two men went up into the temple to pray; one was a Pharisee, and the other was a tax collector. The Pharisee stood and prayed by himself like this: 'God, I thank you that I am not like the rest of men: extortionists, unrighteous, adulterers, or even like this tax collector. I fast twice a week. I give tithes of all that I get.' But the tax collector, standing far away, wouldn't even lift up his eyes to heaven, but beat his chest, saying, 'God, be merciful to me, a sinner!' I tell you, this man went down to his house justified rather than the other; for everyone who exalts himself will be humbled, but he who humbles himself will be exalted." Luke 18:9-14

Reflection:

Jesus warns us about getting too confident in our righteousness. You might think this could never happen to you, but the more you seek Jesus and the closer you get to him, the devil may set a trap of self-righteousness in your path. No matter how close we get to Jesus, we're still sinners, no better than anyone else. Pray to remain humble.

Prayer:

Dear Lord, I want nothing more than to truly know you. The glimpses I see are amazing and make me want more. Please help me remain humble as I seek you. Remind me that I'm a sinner, not worthy of your mercy, and no better than anyone else. I ask this as your humble servant in the name of Jesus, my Lord and Savior. Amen.

They were also bringing their babies to [Jesus], that he might touch them. But when the disciples saw it, they rebuked them. Jesus summoned them, saying, "Allow the little children to come to me, and don't hinder them, for God's Kingdom belongs to such as these. Most certainly, I tell you, whoever doesn't receive God's Kingdom like a little child, he will in no way enter into it." Luke 18:15-17

Reflection:

Children are naturally innocent, trusting, and loving. They cling to their parents and turn to them for everything they need. They love their parents as unconditionally as a human is able, and they never doubt their parents' love. Turn to God as your loving parent. Trust him with your life. Ask him to fulfill your needs and be confident that he will. When we seek Jesus, we offer the best part of ourselves to him, the part that's most like a child.

Prayer:

Lord, I come to you as helpless and needy as a child. I trust you to provide for my needs, and I promise to love you even when your will is different from mine. Teach me how to grow into the disciple you want me to be and give me the grace and strength I need to accomplish your will for me. I pray in the name of Jesus Christ. Amen.

A certain ruler asked [Jesus], saying, "Good Teacher, what shall I do to inherit eternal life?" Jesus asked him, "Why do you call me good? No one is good, except one: God. You know the commandments: 'Don't commit adultery,' 'Don't murder,' 'Don't steal,' 'Don't give false testimony,' 'Honor your father and your mother.'"

He said, "I have observed all these things from my youth up." When Jesus heard these things, he said to him, "You still lack one thing. Sell all that you have and distribute it to the poor. Then you will have treasure in heaven; then come, follow me." But when he heard these things, he became very sad, for he was very rich. Jesus, seeing that he became very sad, said, "How hard it is for those who have riches to enter into God's Kingdom! For it is easier for a camel to enter in through a needle's eye than for a rich man to enter into God's Kingdom."

Those who heard it said, "Then who can be saved?" But he said, "The things which are impossible with men are possible with God." Peter said, "Look, we have left everything and followed you." He said to them, "Most certainly I tell you, there is no one who has left house, or wife, or brothers, or parents, or children, for God's Kingdom's sake, who will not receive many times more in this time, and in the world to come, eternal life." Luke 18:18-30

Reflection:

The magnitude of the requirements Jesus laid out here as necessary to inherit eternal life is scary. It seems impossible when you consider all the ways in which we might fall short. Does it mean we're all doomed and hopeless? Of course not. That would make Jesus' entire ministry on earth worthless. God knows we're fallible. He sets the bar high, but when we seek him, he leads us. When we stay close by his side, we become better Christians, better people, better followers, better disciples. Trust that when you know him as your Lord and Savior, he will welcome you into the Kingdom.

Prayer:

Lord, I am not worthy of you and your Kingdom. I fall short of your requirements. Help me improve my shortcomings, and don't give up on me. Keep nudging me and guiding me to follow your commands. Have mercy on me and my loved ones. I believe that through you, all things are possible, even allowing flawed humans into eternal rest. May all the souls of the faithfully departed, through the mercy of God, rest in peace. Amen.

[Jesus] took the twelve aside and said to them, "Behold, we are going up to Jerusalem, and all the things that are written through the prophets concerning the Son of Man will be completed. For he will be delivered up to the Gentiles, will be mocked, treated shamefully, and spit on. They will scourge and kill him. On the third day, he will rise again." They understood none of these things. This saying was hidden from them, and they didn't understand the things that were said. Luke 18:31-34

Reflection:

What faith the disciples had when Jesus said things they didn't understand. Obviously, they understood enough about his mission and what he represented that they continued to follow and trust him, even when what he said and did didn't make sense to them. We are called to do the same. Sometimes we don't understand why things happen the way they do. Sometimes we can't feel God with us. Sometimes we can't see a way out of a situation. It's at those times we need to remind ourselves that we know Jesus well enough to trust him, even when life seems and feels like gibberish. Trust him even when you don't understand. This is faith.

Prayer:

Lord, when life feels like it's falling apart, it's hard for me to feel you near me. Help me find the trust that the disciples had. I know your hand is at work in my life, and there is light at the end of suffering. Even when I can't understand the meaning or purpose of life's challenges and feel lost and alone, give me the faith to know you're there. Please reveal yourself to me so I know I'm not alone. Turn my heartache into trust. I ask this in the name of Jesus Christ. Amen.

As [Jesus] came near Jericho, a certain blind man sat by the road, begging. Hearing a multitude going by, he asked what this meant. They told him that Jesus of Nazareth was passing by. He cried out, "Jesus, you son of David, have mercy on me!" Those who led the way rebuked him, that he should be quiet; but he cried out all the more, "You son of David, have mercy on me!"

Standing still, Jesus commanded him to be brought to him. When he had come near, he asked him, "What do you want me to do?" He said, "Lord, that I may see again." Jesus said to him, "Receive your sight. Your faith has healed you." Immediately he received his sight and followed him, glorifying God. All the people, when they saw it, praised God. Luke 18:35-43

Reflection:

Jesus again rewards the man who calls out to him in faith. He asks us to rely on him, to believe in him, to put our faith in him. He wants us to bring our desires and needs to him. He wants us to rely on him. He wants us to seek him unabashedly, the way the blind man did.

Prayer:

Dear God, I thank you for the many blessings you've given me in my life. I have faith that you hear me when I talk to you, you care about my wants and needs, and you will never forsake me. You know the hurts in my heart and the ways I need to be healed. I bring all my weaknesses and failings to you and ask for your healing. In Jesus' name. Amen.

❧⫴━━━━━•●•━━━━━⫴❧

[Jesus] entered and was passing through Jericho. There was a man named Zacchaeus. He was a chief tax collector, and he was rich. He was trying to see who Jesus was, and couldn't because of the crowd, because he was short. He ran on ahead and climbed up into a sycamore tree to see him, for he was going to pass that way. When Jesus came to the place, he looked up and saw him, and said to him, "Zacchaeus, hurry and come down, for today I must stay at your house."

He hurried, came down, and received him joyfully. When they saw it, they all murmured, saying, "He has gone in to lodge with a man who is a sinner." Zacchaeus stood and said to the Lord, "Behold, Lord, half of my goods I give to the poor. If I have wrongfully exacted anything of anyone, I restore four times as much." Jesus said to him, "Today, salvation has come to this house, because he also is a son of Abraham. For the Son of Man came to seek and to save that which was lost." Luke 19:1-10

Reflection:

Seek Jesus wholeheartedly like Zacchaeus did! He didn't focus on the obstacles ahead of him; he simply hustled to find a way to get close to Jesus. He didn't worry about what his past was. He didn't worry about not being worthy, and he didn't give up because he couldn't make his way through the crowd. He found a way and just did it. And the transformation in his heart was immediate, with a pledge to give to the poor and make restitution. When we seek Jesus, he welcomes us with open arms, and if we allow him into our hearts, he will transform them.

Prayer:

Dear Lord, thank you for this example of Zacchaeus seeking you. Come into my heart and meet me there. Change me. Make me the disciple you wish me to be. Guide me. Give me the strength and determination to fight off any obstacle that threatens to come between us. I need you. In the holy name of Jesus, Amen.

77

As they heard these things, [Jesus] went on and told a parable, because he was near Jerusalem, and they supposed that God's Kingdom would be revealed immediately.

He said therefore, "A certain nobleman went into a far country to receive for himself a kingdom and to return. He called ten servants of his and gave them ten miña coins, and told them, 'Conduct business until I come.' But his citizens hated him, and sent an envoy after him, saying, 'We don't want this man to reign over us.' When he had come back again, having received the kingdom, he commanded these servants, to whom he had given the money, to be called to him, that he might know what they had gained by conducting business. The first came before him, saying, 'Lord, your miña has made ten more miñas.' He said to him, 'Well done, you good servant! Because you were found faithful with very little, you shall have authority over ten cities.'

"The second came, saying, 'Your miña, Lord, has made five miñas.' So he said to him, 'And you are to be over five cities.' Another came, saying, 'Lord, behold, your miña, which I kept laid away in a handkerchief, for I feared you, because you are an exacting man. You take up that which you didn't lay down, and reap that which you didn't sow.' "He said to him, 'Out of your own mouth I will judge you, you wicked servant! You knew that I am an exacting man, taking up that which I didn't lay down and reaping that which I didn't sow. Then why didn't you deposit my money in the bank, and at my coming, I might have earned interest on it?' He said to those who stood by, 'Take the miña away from him and give it to him who has the ten miñas.'

"They said to him, 'Lord, he has ten miñas!' 'For I tell you that to everyone who has, will more be given; but from him who doesn't have, even that which he has will be taken away from him. But bring those enemies of mine who didn't want me to reign over them here, and kill them before me.'" Luke 19:11-27

Reflection:

God gives each of us spiritual gifts, otherwise known as spiritual superpowers. And he expects us to use them! When we seek Jesus, we get discernment on what those gifts are and how we can use them to advance his Kingdom. Maybe your gift is teaching or evangelism. Maybe it's starting or running a ministry or feeding and clothing the poor. Don't squander your gifts or hide them. Seek Jesus, and he will show you the path he's chosen for you, which will multiply the impact of your gifts. Use your gifts from God to shine his light in the world and draw people to him. Break through any obstacle that's holding you back.

Prayer:

Lord, help me see and embrace the spiritual gifts you've given me. Show me how you want me to use them. Put people and circumstances in my path, so I can be an instrument to advance your Kingdom. Help me trust your plan even when I feel scared, unequipped, or unworthy. I can do anything you request of me with you by my side. Guide me. Amen.

78

Those who were sent went away and found things just as [Jesus] had told them. As they were untying the colt, its owners said to them, "Why are you untying the colt?" They said, "The Lord needs it." Then they brought it to Jesus. They threw their cloaks on the colt and sat Jesus on them. As he went, they spread their cloaks on the road.

As he was now getting near, at the descent of the Mount of Olives, the whole multitude of the disciples began to rejoice and praise God with a loud voice for all the mighty works which they had seen, saying, "Blessed is the King who comes in the name of the Lord! Peace in heaven, and glory in the highest!" Some of the Pharisees from the multitude said to him, "Teacher, rebuke your disciples!" He answered them, "I tell you that if these were silent, the stones would cry out." When he came near, he saw the city and wept over it, saying, "If you, even you, had known today the things which belong to your peace! But now, they are hidden from your eyes." Luke 19:32-42

Reflection:

As Jesus' ministry unfolded and he knew his time on earth was drawing to an end, he had amassed a large following. Yet he wept over those who had refused to see. Jesus loves all his people and hurts for those who won't open their eyes. As seekers of Jesus, we can pray for the eyes of the unseeing to be opened while we continue to encourage those who choose to see.

Prayer:

Dear Heavenly Father, because you love us, you gave us the beautiful gift of free will. But it means people can choose not to follow you, and you won't force them. Please send the Holy Spirit to breathe your truth into their hearts. Loudly and often. Open their ears, speak to their hearts, and show them the way to you. Reveal yourself to them. Give them signs. Please don't give up on the lost. I ask this in the name of your Son, Jesus Christ. Amen.

[Jesus] entered into the temple and began to drive out those who bought and sold in it, saying to them, "It is written, 'My house is a house of prayer,' but you have made it a 'den of robbers'!"

He was teaching daily in the temple, but the chief priests, the scribes, and the leading men among the people sought to destroy him. They couldn't find what they might do, for all the people hung on to every word that he said. Luke 19:45-48

Reflection:

As a human, Jesus must have feared. He knew the leaders were trying to find a reason to kill him. But it didn't stop him from living out his ministry. When we do the work of God, he protects us. He gives us the strength to continue even in the face of adversity. And he assures us that any harm that comes our way is worth the cost. Jesus knew what the outcome of his ministry would be. Maybe we don't know the outcome of God's will for our lives, but we can always trust that his perfect plan will have an amazing outcome, even as we face tremendous struggles.

Prayer:

Lord, I trust in your perfect plan for my life. I lay my burdens at your feet and ask you to use me to advance your Kingdom. I'm scared and nervous about what you might call me to do, but I know you'll never leave my side and will give me everything I need. Help me be a warrior for the Kingdom. In Jesus' name. Amen.

~ *80* ~

On one of those days, as [Jesus] was teaching the people in the temple and preaching the Good News, the priests and scribes came to him with the elders. They asked him, "Tell us: by what authority do you do these things? Or who is giving you this authority?" He answered them, "I also will ask you one question. Tell me: the baptism of John, was it from heaven, or from men?"

They reasoned with themselves, saying, "If we say, 'From heaven,' he will say, 'Why didn't you believe him?' But if we say, 'From men,' all the people will stone us, for they are persuaded that John was a prophet." They answered that they didn't know where it was from. Jesus said to them, "Neither will I tell you by what authority I do these things." Luke 21:1-8

Reflection:

The local leaders were determined to find a way to trip Jesus up and use that as the reason to persecute him. Jesus didn't fall for it. We can use his example in our own lives. When faced with religious opposition, call upon the Holy Spirit to give you the correct responses. Don't allow yourself to be baited into no-win situations.

Prayer:

Dear Lord, give me the right words to bring your message to other believers and stand up to nonbelievers. I can only draw people to you if you guide me. Give me signs when I should speak out, and tell me when to move on. Even though I might not feel qualified, I know you will help me accomplish anything you need from me. I trust you. Amen.

[Jesus] began to tell the people this parable: "A man planted a vineyard and rented it out to some farmers, and went into another country for a long time. At the proper season, he sent a servant to the farmers to collect his share of the fruit of the vineyard. But the farmers beat him and sent him away empty. He sent yet another servant, and they also beat him and treated him shamefully, and sent him away empty. He sent yet a third, and they also wounded him and threw him out. The lord of the vineyard said, 'What shall I do? I will send my beloved son. It may be that seeing him, they will respect him.'

"But when the farmers saw him, they reasoned among themselves, saying, 'This is the heir. Come, let's kill him, that the inheritance may be ours.' Then they threw him out of the vineyard and killed him. What therefore will the lord of the vineyard do to them? He will come and destroy these farmers, and will give the vineyard to others." When they heard that, they said, "May that never be!" Luke 20:9-16

Reflection:

Jesus knew he would be giving up his life and included himself in the parable, as represented by the son the tenants killed. And he's also telling us through this parable that we're the servants God sends to retrieve his fruit. He warns us we may be shamed, beaten, or thrown out. It can be a daunting thought to follow where God leads us, but when we seek him, we develop a close, trusting relationship that makes the bumpy roads ahead seem easier to navigate. Stay close to him, and you will always have the strength to handle adversity that comes your way.

Prayer:

Dear Jesus, you provided an amazing example for Christians to follow. Sometimes the message is hard to hear. I get scared and nervous about the path you've laid ahead of me, but I want to do your will. Grant me the strength and determination to do anything you ask of me. Travel this road with me. Never leave my side. I need you. Amen.

The chief priests and the scribes sought to lay hands on [Jesus] that very hour, but they feared the people—for they knew he had spoken this parable against them. Luke 20:19

Reflection:

You're probably familiar with the phrase, "Don't kill the messenger." This is the exact situation Jesus found himself facing. The teachers of the law and chief priests were offended by the things Jesus was saying. Our calling as Christians is to stand up for the message, that is, to spread God's Word. People who don't believe or who are living against the will of God will want to kill the messenger. Ask for God's grace and guidance when you find yourself facing opposition. Jesus instructed others to brush the dust off their shoes and walk away when faced with those who refused to believe. At some point, we're supposed to pick up and move on. Pray for discernment when you find yourself facing opposition.

Prayer:

Dear Heavenly Father, I want to help draw people to your Kingdom. Please help me stay humble so I don't become judgmental and turn them away from you. You are the only judge. Tell me when to pursue and when to let go. Give me the right words to say. Send the Holy Spirit to guide me. I ask this in the name of Jesus Christ, my Lord and Savior. Amen.

They watched [Jesus] and sent out spies, who pretended to be righteous, that they might trap him in something he said, so as to deliver him up to the power and authority of the governor. They asked him, "Teacher, we know that you say and teach what is right, and aren't partial to anyone, but truly teach the way of God. Is it lawful for us to pay taxes to Caesar, or not?"

But he perceived their craftiness, and said to them, "Why do you test me? Show me a denarius. Whose image and inscription are on it?" They answered, "Caesar's." He said to them, "Then give to Caesar the things that are Caesar's, and to God the things that are God's." They weren't able to trap him in his words before the people. They marveled at his answer and were silent. Luke 20:20-26

Reflection:

As his opponents grew more desperate to try to prove Jesus guilty of a crime, they asked him a trick question, thinking they could use his answer against him. He knew what they were doing and that they weren't giving up. Still, Jesus maintained his composure. When we read the words of the Gospel, it doesn't sound so difficult, but imagine what their badgering actually felt like to Jesus. How angry or frustrated do you get when someone baits you and is intentionally trying to trip you up? Pray for the right words, and they will come. Remain calm. Let God speak through you.

Prayer:

Jesus, you were treated unfairly and you knew it. Yet you remained calm and strong and never relented. Grant me a fraction of your resolve and strength. Help me speak out for you. Give me the words. Show me the way. Amen.

84

Some of the Sadducees came to [Jesus], those who deny that there is a resurrection. They asked him, "Teacher, Moses wrote to us that if a man's brother dies having a wife, and he is childless, his brother should take the wife and raise up children for his brother. There were therefore seven brothers. The first took a wife, and died childless. The second took her as wife, and he died childless. The third took her, and likewise the seven all left no children, and died. Afterward the woman also died. Therefore in the resurrection whose wife of them will she be? For the seven had her as a wife." Jesus said to them, "The children of this age marry and are given in marriage. But those who are considered worthy to attain to that age and the resurrection from the dead neither marry nor are given in marriage. For they can't die any more, for they are like the angels and are children of God, being children of the resurrection." Luke 20:27-36

Reflection:

Jesus' answer to the Sadducees gives us a rare and beautiful glimpse into the Kingdom of God. We sometimes wonder what heaven will be like, and we tend to judge it by earthly practices and conditions, because that's all we know. But Jesus' explanation about marriage in heaven is yet one more example of God's perfect plan. In heaven, there will be no jealousy or competition, so God must have designed a way to make it harmonious for everyone. Even when we can't fathom the structure within the heavenly Kingdom, we can rest assured that there is not one detail God overlooked. He has it all under control. With his perfect plan, we will have nothing to fear once we are welcomed into the gates.

Prayer:

Dear God, I can't help but wonder what heaven is like, and I thank you for the glimpses you've given us of what awaits. It's beyond my comprehension. Help me to trust you and lay at your feet my anxiety and worry about what's to come. Help me focus instead on staying the course that will lead me to you. I can't wait to see the Kingdom and be reunited with my loved ones. But first, help me live my remaining days seeking you. I love you always and pray in the name of Jesus. Amen.

In the hearing of all the people, [Jesus] said to his disciples, "Beware of those scribes who like to walk in long robes, and love greetings in the marketplaces, the best seats in the synagogues, and the best places at feasts; who devour widows' houses, and for a pretense make long prayers. These will receive greater condemnation." Luke 20:45-47

Reflection:

Jesus warned against impostors. These are the opposite of seekers. Impostors are righteous on the outside but hollow on the inside. When Jesus asks us to seek him, it has little to do with what people can actually see. It all begins in the heart and flows outward from there.

Prayer:

Dear Heavenly Father, help me focus more on keeping you in my heart than on doing things people expect of me. Fill my hollow heart with you. Reveal yourself to me in my heart, mind, and soul. Pull me back when I start drifting away. Help me become an example for others of the amazing joy that comes from truly knowing and seeking you. Without you, I am nothing. Pour your spirit into me. I ask this in the name of Jesus, the Savior of the world. Amen.

[Jesus] looked up and saw the rich people who were putting their gifts into the treasury. He saw a certain poor widow casting in two small brass coins. He said, "Truly I tell you, this poor widow put in more than all of them, for all these put in gifts for God from their abundance, but she, out of her poverty, put in all that she had to live on." Luke 21:1-4

Reflection:

Many of us give money to the church and to the needy. But do we give even when it's difficult? When we give out of our surplus, even if it's a hefty contribution, the heavenly value is not as great as when we give out of what we have to live on. Those giving out of surplus should consider some soul-searching. When we seek Jesus, He's not asking for our scraps. He's asking to be our priority as we are his priority. When we trust in him, he will never forsake us. We can entrust our wealth to him.

Prayer:

Dear Lord, I want to seek you, but I still hold on to some of my human failings, especially regarding money. I sometimes fret over financial security and how much money is enough for a secure future. I fall into the temptation of buying fancy things for the sake of buying them. I spend money frivolously on silly pleasures that society convinces me I need. Grant me the strength to keep money in its place and not allow it to become an idol. Assure me that I can give generously to you and the needy, and you will not forsake me in my time of need. Help me lay my fears and reservations at your feet and use money to help advance your Kingdom. In Jesus' name. Amen.

There will be signs in the sun, moon, and stars; and on the earth anxiety of nations, in perplexity for the roaring of the sea and the waves; men fainting for fear and for expectation of the things which are coming on the world, for the powers of the heavens will be shaken. Then they will see the Son of Man coming in a cloud with power and great glory. But when these things begin to happen, look up and lift up your heads, because your redemption is near. So be careful, or your hearts will be loaded down with carousing, drunkenness, and cares of this life, and that day will come on you suddenly. For it will come like a snare on all those who dwell on the surface of all the earth. Therefore be watchful all the time, praying that you may be counted worthy to escape all these things that will happen, and to stand before the Son of Man. Luke 21:25-28, 34-36

Reflection:

Jesus warns us about letting our guard down and being unprepared for when our time on Earth ends. When we seek him, we're as prepared as we can be for whenever our day of judgment comes. When we seek him, we make choices to reject the traps of society that might otherwise pull us away from him. When we keep our hearts full of Jesus, we make choices out of love for him, not out of fear of punishment.

Prayer:

Dear God, I love to imagine your heavenly Kingdom, and I pray my faith is enough to spend eternity with you. Please keep me and my loved ones by your side and never let us stray. Fill my heart with your love and help me live my life as an example that draws others to you. Grant me your grace to live my life fully for you, so I'm prepared to stand before you at the end. I ask this in the name of Jesus Christ. Amen.

88

Now the feast of unleavened bread, which is called the Passover, was approaching. The chief priests and the scribes sought how they might put [Jesus] to death, for they feared the people.

Satan entered into Judas, who was also called Iscariot, who was counted with the twelve. He went away and talked with the chief priests and captains about how he might deliver him to them. They were glad, and agreed to give him money. He consented and sought an opportunity to deliver him to them in the absence of the multitude. Luke 22:1-6

Reflection:

We don't like to think about evil, but it exists. Satan is always trying to weasel his way into our hearts and minds. He's a smooth talker and very convincing. The apostles had spent nearly three years following Jesus and had given up their lives for him, so it would seem logical that they were loyal to him, but Judas proved otherwise. He acted like a supporter and friend, but his heart wasn't in it. Judas had a hollow relationship with Jesus, like ours can become when we don't seek him. Don't let Satan find a weak spot to attack your heart or soul. Seeking Jesus and keeping him ever-present in thought, word, and deed keeps Satan at bay.

Prayer:

Dear Heavenly Father, the last thing I want to do is make choices that drive wedges between us. Keep my mind clear of worldly desires and full of you and your love so there are no temptations that can lead me away from you. Nudge me when I'm letting my guard down. Pull me back when I start drifting. Protect me and my loved ones from the power of evil and lead us not into temptation. I ask this in the holy name of Jesus. Amen.

89

When the hour had come, [Jesus] sat down with the twelve apostles. He said to them, "I have earnestly desired to eat this Passover with you before I suffer, for I tell you, I will no longer by any means eat of it until it is fulfilled in God's Kingdom." He received a cup, and when he had given thanks, he said, "Take this and share it among yourselves, for I tell you, I will not drink at all again from the fruit of the vine, until God's Kingdom comes."

He took bread, and when he had given thanks, he broke and gave it to them, saying, "This is my body which is given for you. Do this in memory of me." Likewise, he took the cup after supper, saying, "This cup is the new covenant in my blood, which is poured out for you. But behold, the hand of him who betrays me is with me on the table. The Son of Man indeed goes as it has been determined, but woe to that man through whom he is betrayed!" They began to question among themselves which of them it was who would do this thing. Luke 22:14-23

Reflection:

It's painful to think that Jesus knew it was his last supper and foresaw the torture he would face after betrayal by a former supporter. He used the opportunity to give us the beautiful gift of communion that we celebrate in Christian churches today. More than two thousand years later, we can be transported back to that upper room, sitting at the table with Jesus and sharing the bread and wine of his body that he offered for us. He speaks to you and me in holy communion. Imagine yourself with the disciples in that room, accepting his body and blood. Carry this feeling with you each time you receive communion.

Prayer:

Dear Jesus, sometimes I lose sight of all that you sacrificed for me. Thank you for giving me the gift of your body and blood that nourishes my heart and soul and reminds me of your love for your people. I'm not worthy of your love and your sacrifice. Help me follow your example to use my life and talents to the best of my ability to further the holy Kingdom. I love you. Amen.

90

[Jesus] came out and went, as his custom was, to the Mount of Olives. His disciples also followed him. When he was at the place, he said to them, "Pray that you don't enter into temptation."

He was withdrawn from them about a stone's throw, and he knelt down and prayed, saying, "Father, if you are willing, remove this cup from me. Nevertheless, not my will, but yours, be done." An angel from heaven appeared to him, strengthening him. Being in agony, he prayed more earnestly. His sweat became like great drops of blood falling down on the ground.

When he rose up from his prayer, he came to the disciples and found them sleeping because of grief, and said to them, "Why do you sleep? Rise and pray that you may not enter into temptation." Luke 22:39-46

Reflection:

You may have heard this message so many times that you may have become indifferent or numb to the anguish Jesus felt. We can take for granted that he gave his life for us, but when we seek him, we put ourselves in his shoes. As a human, He was scared, he was hurting, and he dreaded going through it. *Feel* that. Put yourself in his sandals. He was drenched in sweat and blood from his anguish. He was let down by the sleeping disciples when he needed their support. His reaction was fully human, and we can relate. Jesus provides the best example possible for us in taking up the cross we've been given in life, by saying, "Father, if you are willing, take this cup from me; yet not my will, but yours be done." When we seek him, we ask for our desires as humans, but we choose his will over our own.

Prayer:

Dear Heavenly Father, you let your Son suffer the consequences for human sin. How difficult it must have been to see him in agony. Thank you for providing salvation for your people, even when it meant sacrificing your beloved one. We are not worthy of what you've done for us. You sacrificed Jesus for me and everyone throughout the world. Help me use my life by continuing the work Jesus started. Lead me to where you need me. I love you. Amen.

While [Jesus] was still speaking, a crowd appeared. He who was called Judas, one of the twelve, was leading them. He came near to Jesus to kiss him. But Jesus said to him, "Judas, do you betray the Son of Man with a kiss?" Luke 22:47-48

Reflection:

Because of his divinity, Jesus knew Judas would betray him. But he was also fully human, so we can assume the heartache that the betrayal caused him as Judas approached. His response to Judas sounds very nonchalant, but imagine the anguish of being stabbed in the back by someone who pretended to be your good friend. If ever we think Jesus can't understand our pain and our grief, remember everything he went through to save us. He certainly understands how hard life can be.

Prayer:

Jesus, as your ministry on earth was coming to an end, you faced so much pain and loss. I'm sorry that human sin caused you so much anguish. I'm eternally thankful that you came to save us. Not only are you an amazing God, but you also understand the hurt, disappointment, and fears of humans because you've experienced it all. I can't comprehend your depth. I know that with you by my side, I can accomplish anything I'm called to do. Thank you for loving me. I love you. Amen.

[Peter] denied Jesus, saying, "Woman, I don't know him." After a little while someone else saw him and said, "You also are one of them!" But Peter answered, "Man, I am not!"

After about one hour passed, another confidently affirmed, saying, "Truly this man also was with him, for he is a Galilean!" But Peter said, "Man, I don't know what you are talking about!" Immediately, while he was still speaking, a rooster crowed. The Lord turned and looked at Peter. Then Peter remembered the Lord's word, how he said to him, "Before the rooster crows you will deny me three times." He went out, and wept bitterly. Luke 22:57-62

Reflection:

How many times do we regret our reaction when faced with a question or situation that caught us off guard? You probably have at least one example that you wish you could do over. Peter was one of Jesus' greatest supporters, yet he still stumbled when the going got tough. It was certainly easier for Peter to deny Jesus than to face the same punishment if he acknowledged knowing him. Peter's denial reminds us that we're humans and we don't handle every situation perfectly. But we can also learn that when we seek Jesus and keep him firmly in our hearts, we're best prepared to face challenges to our faith and ready to speak out on his behalf.

Prayer:

Dear Father in Heaven, forgive me when I fail you like Peter did. Forgive me when I take the easier path or the one with less controversy. Teach me instead to rely on your strength to stand up for you and everything the Kingdom represents. Place the words to use on my lips. Put me in the path of people who need to hear the words. Lead me according to your will. Amen.

The men who held Jesus mocked him and beat him. Having blind-folded him, they struck him on the face and asked him, "Prophesy! Who is the one who struck you?" They spoke many other things against him, insulting him. Luke 22:63-65

Reflection:

Now Jesus was all alone with his tormentors. His disciples and other supporters had scattered. As fully divine, Jesus had the benefit of knowing there was light on the other side of his darkest hours. When we're in the depths of darkness, like Jesus was, we can't see what's on the other side, and it can feel like there's nothing but darkness ahead. Seek Jesus in your darkest hour. See him in your mind's eye. Feel his love surround you. Remind yourself that God's plan is perfect. There is always sunshine after a storm. Trust him.

Prayer:

Dear Lord, speak to me loudly when I'm lost in the darkness of life's challenges. Walk beside me. Give me faith to know you've not deserted me and that the sun will shine again. Remind me that you have the perfect plan and you are watching out for me. Stay in my heart and never let me go. I need you. Amen.

As soon as it was day, the assembly of the elders of the people were gathered together, both chief priests and scribes, and they led [Jesus] away into their council, saying, "If you are the Christ, tell us." But he said to them, "If I tell you, you won't believe, and if I ask, you will in no way answer me or let me go. From now on, the Son of Man will be seated at the right hand of the power of God."

They all said, "Are you then the Son of God?" He said to them, "You say it, because I am." They said, "Why do we need any more witness? For we ourselves have heard from his own mouth!" Luke 22:66-71

Reflection:

As humans, we tend to try proving our points to the bitter end. We get indignant when we are falsely accused. We strike out when we're backed into a corner. Jesus reminds us that at some point it's prudent to acknowledge and accept when people aren't open to hearing the truth and when they're closed-minded to a different opinion. Seek discernment from Jesus to know when to speak out, when to back down, or when to simply shake the dust off your sandals and move on.

Prayer:

Dear Lord, I want to help draw people to your Kingdom, but I need you to guide me. Show me when you want me to be persistent and when you want me to move on. Lead me. Give me confidence to overcome my fears. Help me live my life as an example of what being a Christian means. I ask this in the name of Jesus. Amen.

There were also others, two criminals, led with [Jesus] to be put to death. When they came to the place that is called "The Skull", they crucified him there with the criminals, one on the right and the other on the left. Jesus said, "Father, forgive them, for they don't know what they are doing."

Dividing his garments among them, they cast lots. The people stood watching. The rulers with them also scoffed at him, saying, "He saved others. Let him save himself, if this is the Christ of God, his chosen one!" The soldiers also mocked him, coming to him and offering him vinegar, and saying, "If you are the King of the Jews, save yourself!" An inscription was also written over him in letters of Greek, Latin, and Hebrew: "THIS IS THE KING OF THE JEWS." One of the criminals who was hanged insulted him, saying, "If you are the Christ, save yourself and us!"

But the other answered, and rebuking him said, "Don't you even fear God, seeing you are under the same condemnation? And we indeed justly, for we receive the due reward for our deeds, but this man has done nothing wrong." He said to Jesus, "Lord, remember me when you come into your Kingdom." Jesus said to him, "Assuredly I tell you, today you will be with me in Paradise." Luke 23:32-43

Reflection:

This long passage is packed with amazing points for reflection, so go back and read it again if you need to savor each bit. Let's now focus on the incredible hope that Jesus gave us by forgiving and welcoming the criminal the moment he showed faith. We have seen this many times over the course of Jesus' ministry, except in this passage, he's dying. He's being taunted while bleeding and suffocating at the hands of tormentors. Yet God's love has no limits. Even during the most brutal and tragic circumstances, God's love shines. His forgiveness is simply waiting for us

Prayer:

Jesus, my heart breaks at the thought of you being tortured and killed for me. I can never be worthy of such a sacrifice that you made. Your love and forgiveness are beyond the limits of my understanding. I pray that my faith has been enough to celebrate eternity with you when my time on earth is over. Forgive me when I disappoint you. Please never give up on your people. I ask this in your holy name. Amen.

It was now about the sixth hour, and darkness came over the whole land until the ninth hour. The sun was darkened, and the veil of the temple was torn in two. Jesus, crying with a loud voice, said, "Father, into your hands I commit my spirit!" Having said this, he breathed his last. Luke 23:44-46

Reflection:

Imagine sacrificing your child's life for people who were sinners, disobedient, and disloyal. Imagine willingly giving up your own life for those same people. On a human level, we wouldn't even consider it. This shows just how amazing the love of God the Father and Jesus is: that the Father would sacrifice his Son's life for sinners and that Jesus would accept the torment of his Father's will. We can't grasp the amount of love those acts represent, but seeking Jesus with our whole heart is the least we can do in response.

Prayer:

Dear God, I give you all glory, honor, and praise now and forever. I'm unworthy of the love you've given me. There's no way I can offer you a fraction of that love in return, but help me honor you by living my life in accordance with your perfect will. I'm a sinner who doesn't deserve the ultimate sacrifice you made for me, but I pray to stand before you someday in your heavenly Kingdom. I pray in the name of Jesus, my Savior. Amen.

But on the first day of the week, at early dawn, they and some others came to the tomb, bringing the spices which they had prepared. They found the stone rolled away from the tomb. They entered in, and didn't find the Lord Jesus' body. While they were greatly perplexed about this, behold, two men stood by them in dazzling clothing. Becoming terrified, they bowed their faces down to the earth. The men said to them, "Why do you seek the living among the dead? He isn't here, but is risen. Remember what he told you when he was still in Galilee, saying that the Son of Man must be delivered up into the hands of sinful men and be crucified, and the third day rise again?"

They remembered his words, returned from the tomb, and told all these things to the eleven and to all the rest. Now they were Mary Magdalene, Joanna, and Mary the mother of James. The other women with them told these things to the apostles. These words seemed to them to be nonsense, and they didn't believe them. But Peter got up and ran to the tomb. Stooping and looking in, he saw the strips of linen lying by themselves, and he departed to his home, wondering what had happened. Luke 24:1-12

Reflection:

Alleluia! He is Risen! What a beautiful (and frightening) experience it must have been for the women at the tomb. Imagine their joy and amazement when the confusing things that Jesus had told them began to come into focus. Today, we can celebrate the resurrection with the same joy and amazement. Jesus conquered death to save us. The torture that he endured resulted in the greatest gift we will ever receive. Remember the beauty that resulted from Jesus' suffering when you're in the midst of your own darkness.

Prayer:

Dear Heavenly Father, the gift of your Son that resulted in his death and resurrection is an act of love beyond measure. Help me trust in your perfect will and surrender my life to it, so Jesus' death was not in vain. I love you. Amen.

98

Behold, two of them were going that very day to a village named Emmaus, which was sixty stadia from Jerusalem. They talked with each other about all of these things which had happened. While they talked and questioned together, Jesus himself came near, and went with them. But their eyes were kept from recognizing him. He said to them, "What are you talking about as you walk, and are sad?"

One of them, named Cleopas, answered him, "Are you the only stranger in Jerusalem who doesn't know the things which have happened there in these days?" He said to them, "What things?" They said to him, "The things concerning Jesus the Nazarene, who was a prophet mighty in deed and word before God and all the people; and how the chief priests and our rulers delivered him up to be condemned to death, and crucified him. But we were hoping that it was he who would redeem Israel. Yes, and besides all this, it is now the third day since these things happened. Also, certain women of our company amazed us, having arrived early at the tomb; and when they didn't find his body, they came saying that they had also seen a vision of angels, who said that he was alive. Some of us went to the tomb and found it just like the women had said, but they didn't see him." He said to them, "Foolish people, and slow of heart to believe in all that the prophets have spoken! Didn't the Christ have to suffer these things and to enter into his glory?" Beginning from Moses and from all the prophets, he explained to them in all the Scriptures the things concerning himself.

They came near to the village where they were going, and he acted like he would go further. They urged him, saying, "Stay with us, for it is almost evening, and the day is almost over." He went in to stay with them. When he had sat down at the table with them, he took the bread and gave thanks. Breaking it, he gave it to them. Their eyes were opened and they recognized him; then he vanished out of their sight. They said to one another, "Weren't our hearts burning within us while he spoke to us along the way, and while he opened the Scriptures to us?" They rose up that very hour, returned to Jerusalem, and found the eleven gathered together, and those who were with them, saying, "The Lord is risen indeed, and has appeared to Simon!" They related the things that happened along the way, and how he was recognized by them in the breaking of the bread. Luke 24:13-35

Reflection:

This miraculous experience on the road to Emmaus reminds us that God is among us. Are your eyes open to see him? Are your ears listening for him? Jesus presents himself to us in everyday ways. Are you paying attention? Are you seeking him?

Prayer:

Jesus, help me pay attention to the ways you present yourself to me. Open my eyes to see, my ears to hear, and my heart to feel. Meet me when I seek you. I'm your servant forever. Amen.

99

As they said these things, Jesus himself stood among them, and said to them, "Peace be to you." But they were terrified and filled with fear, and supposed that they had seen a spirit. He said to them, "Why are you troubled? Why do doubts arise in your hearts? See my hands and my feet, that it is truly me. Touch me and see, for a spirit doesn't have flesh and bones, as you see that I have." When he had said this, he showed them his hands and his feet. While they still didn't believe for joy, and wondered, he said to them, "Do you have anything here to eat?" They gave him a piece of a broiled fish and some honeycomb. He took them, and ate in front of them. He said to them, "This is what I told you while I was still with you, that all things which are written in the law of Moses, the prophets, and the psalms concerning me must be fulfilled."

Then he opened their minds, that they might understand the Scriptures. He said to them, "Thus it is written, and thus it was necessary for the Christ to suffer and to rise from the dead the third day, and that repentance and remission of sins should be preached in his name to all the nations, beginning at Jerusalem. You are witnesses of these things." Luke 24:36-48

Reflection:

Jesus did everything to prove his resurrection, yet people still doubted. Jesus said that those who haven't seen and still believe are blessed. That's the challenge for today's Christians. Firm up your faith by seeking Jesus. He will show himself to you.

Prayer:

Jesus, you revealed your resurrection in beautiful and miraculous ways. Grant me the faith to stand firmly on your Word. Reveal yourself to me when doubt creeps in and let me be an instrument that draws others to you. Amen.

100

[Jesus] led them out as far as Bethany, and he lifted up his hands and blessed them. While he blessed them, he withdrew from them and was carried up into heaven. They worshiped him and returned to Jerusalem with great joy, and were continually in the temple, praising and blessing God. Amen. Luke 24:50-53

Reflection:

What a mind-blowing experience it must have been for those who witnessed Jesus' bodily ascension to heaven. Put yourself there in your mind. This is God revealing himself to his people. It's Jesus proving that he fulfilled what was written in the scriptures. How do we keep that great joy alive today? Yes, by seeking him.

Prayer:

Lord, help me seek you. Burn a fire in my heart. Give me the strength to value your love over the temptations of the world. Reveal your plan for me. Walk with me and give me the strength to accomplish it. I am nothing without you. I am forever your child. In the most holy name of Jesus, the almighty Savior of the World. Amen.

Thank you!

Thank you for taking this spiritual journey through the Gospel of Luke. I pray that it has helped deepen your faith and strengthen your relationship with Jesus. I hope it has inspired you to continue seeking him with your whole heart.

Have you read my other book, **Divine Wisdom** – *Life Lessons from the Parables of Jesus*? It follows a similar format to this devotional, but delves into greater detail and explanation for 40 of Jesus' life-changing parables. If you liked this devotional, you'll like that one even more! Check it out.

If you enjoyed this devotional, I would be so grateful if you would leave a short review on Amazon. Your words not only mean the world to me, but they also help other readers discover this book, too. Thank you in advance for being willing to share your thoughts!

May the Lord bless and keep you.
May He make his face to shine on you and be gracious to you.
May He lift up his face toward you and give you peace.

—Numbers 6:24-26

www.ingramcontent.com/pod-product-compliance
Lightning Source LLC
Chambersburg PA
CBHW061722020426
42331CB00006B/1055